I0786035

ISBN-13:
978-1725721975

ISBN-10:
172572197X

DRAG411's Ten Black Books

Book 1:	**DRAG411's "DRAG Bully, A Survivor's Guide"**
	Copyright © 2015 and 2018
Book 2:	**DRAG411's "Original DRAG Handbook"**
	Copyright © 2010, 2011, 2012, 2014, and 2018
Book 3:	**DRAG411's "Crown Me! Winning Pageants"**
	Copyright © 2013, 2014, and 2018
Book 4:	**DRAG411's "DRAG King Guide"**
	Copyright © 2014 and 2018
Book 5:	**DRAG411's "DRAG Stories"**
	Copyright © 2011, 2014, and 2018
Book 6:	**DRAG411's "DRAG Mother, DRAG Father"**
	Copyright © 2012, 2014, and 2018
Book 7:	**DRAG411's "Spotlight Today"**
	Copyright © 2012 and 2018
Book 8:	**DRAG411's "DRAG Queen Guide"**
	Copyright © 2014 and 2018
Book 9:	Two Comedy Scripts:
	DRAG411's "Best Said Dead"
	Copyright © 2011, 2014, and 2018
	"Following Wynter"
	Copyright © 2012, 2014, and 2018
Book 10:	**DRAG411's "DRAG World"**
	Copyright © 2012 and 2018

From the best-selling author of "CommUnity of Transition,"
"Two Days Past Dead," The Novel and the sequel,
"Turn Around Bright Eyes, The DRAG Queen Killer,"
"Joey Brooks, The Show Must Go On," and
"Waiting On God."

DRAG
WORLD
.ORG
World's Largest Magazine for Impersonators and Fans
Come Out,
Come Out,
Wherever
You Are
FREE
Summer 2012

DRAG411's

❀ ❀ ❀

DRAG
World

2nd Edition

I am not a fan of the term "DRAG" as applied across this entire art form, but until they find a single word "more accepting," I will have to use it. The DRAG community has helped me earn twenty LGBT world records. I created DRAG411 to document this form of entertainment. We are the world's largest organization for male, female, and androgynous impersonators with over 7,000 current or former impersonators in 32 countries.   Todd   Kachinski Kottmeier

(sic)

Latin adverb: thus"; in full: sic erat scriptum, thus was it written indicates DRAG411 transcribed the comments into this book exactly as found in the original source, complete with any erroneous or archaic spelling or other nonstandard presentation. We try to print the responses using the same words sent to us, ensuring the reader DRAG411 did not change the tone, reflection, or character of each response.

We print verbatim, without editing

ver·ba·tim   vərˈbātəm/
adverb: verbatim; adjective
in exactly the same words as used originally.

Go to our website at
DRAG411.com
to locate any name listed
in any of the books
in our Ten Black Book series
and the details of each
book, entertainer,
and chapter.

Steve's Carpet Cleaning
Carpet, Tile,
Pressure Washing,
Upholstery, Grout
Cleaning, and
Emergency
Water Extraction
Serving Pinellas,
Pasco, and
Hillsborough
Counties Seven
Days a week,
23 hours
a day!
(727) 251.4039
Click this advertisement
To open our website without
Leaving the security of facebook!
StevesCarpet.com

Note: Spotlight Today became Drag World Magazine at print. Most of the email addresses and links no longer work (except for DRAG411.com).

Thousands of entertainers perform across the country as kings, queens, androgynous performers, female to male (FTM), male to female (MTF), and as impersonators. In history, no date in record has more impersonators than today. Tomorrow this record will break. Not only will today's record be broken, but also by the end of the month, tomorrow's record amount of performers will be a distant memory. Each day dozens of boys and girls are considering cross-dressing for the sole purpose of stealing the limelight, capturing the undivided attention of a crowded room; for the opportunity to perform a song that only the day before they relegated to lip synching from the front seat of their car.

Less than twenty entertainers in the entire world will earn a good living solely on their own, using the revenue exclusively from performing. No matter what a pretentious queen tells you about rejecting fans that try to give them dollar bills... this is a dollar trade that even the most glorious performers in the country will tell you, they earn one dollar at a time. The average impersonator works a mainstream job and/or shares expenses with another person to make ends meet.

I repeat this quote of twenty entertainers, though our massive archives of over 5,600 impersonators places the actual figure at four people in the entire nation claiming the past ten years they lived alone, supporting themselves solely on performing. With the increase of supply, exceeding demand, the pay rates will continue to diminish for even the highest paid entertainers.

This summer's cover story will not be having me discussing the best way to make more money. I am not qualified to share those secrets. I do not have the slightest idea on better ways to apply makeup, purchase

wigs, lip synch, select wardrobe outfits, back flip, or the best application of duct tape. I have thousands of more qualified entertainers to share these steps with you in each issue of *Spotlight Today* Magazine.

Only a dozen Master Marketers exist in the field of impersonation throughout the entire world. A marketer is not a promoter. A marketer's duties include the identification of the goods and services desired by a set of consumers, as well as the marketing of those goods and services on behalf of a company. For those of you that do not have the slightest idea who I am, I am a Master Marketer, and this column is to teach you how to market yourself better. My best proof of showing you how good I am at marketing... you are reading my book. I want you to read this entire column with authority, so let me waste two more minutes explaining my credentials so you will take me seriously (starting with me, cutting my skills down).

I do not know much about dressing as the opposite sex. I struggle hard enough through life trying to manage not looking like a male dork. I am sure my boyfriend, that by the way does dress in drag, will tell you by looking at my clothes... that I am still a nerd. With the help of wonderful friends, with incredible talents, and my Senior Editor, Steve Hammond, to give me confidence, I now own the largest drag company on earth. I don't like to use the word DrAG (Dressed As Girl), but it is the only word generally accepted as identifiable by both men and women for this craft.

In 2010, thousands of impersonators reached into their hearts and minds to offer wisdom and insight to help me write my second best seller, "The Official Drag Handbook." The data collected was so immense,

from so many performers, that not only did it break every GLBTQ record, but it also packed out my living room with crates of documents. In all, it broke three world records and inspired other performers to tap into the book's tour premise to create

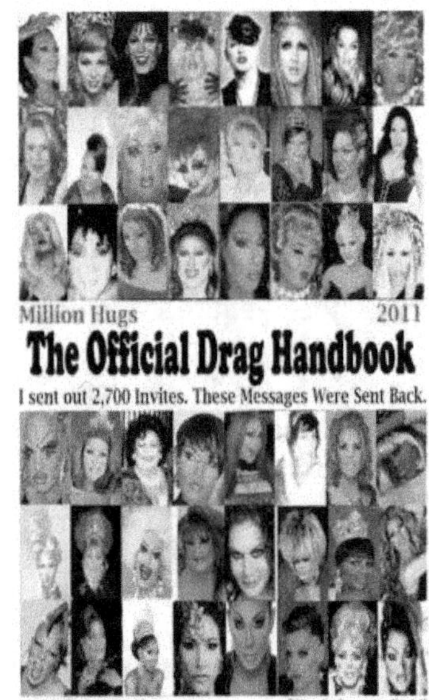

One event alone on June 2, 2011, produced by Iain St. James, packed the Epic Event Center in the Twin cities, with over 167 impersonators invited to take

to the stage for the event. By the end of the night, they landed in the Guinness Book of World Records.

Talk about marketing!

Rolling off the success of the Official Drag Handbook, came volume one of "Drag Stories," followed by the first book in history on mentoring, "Drag Parents," with over 140 impersonators honoring those people in their lives. Even the premiere of *Spotlight Today* Magazine crushed long held international records.

Marketing.

Now with all the self-glorification crap out of the way and off my resume, I hope I have convinced you enough to value my column designed to make you marketable. Guerrilla marketing uses low cost creative strategies of marketing utilizing time, energy, and imagination and not financial resources. Incredible opportunities for marketing develop each day.

I am fortunate enough to

have the largest database in the world to share with you in each issue, and in each book, to assist you in creating the best path for your career as an impersonator. Mind the word career. The Oxford English Dictionary defines a career as a person's "course or progress through life or a distinct portion of life." It can also pertain to an occupation or a profession that usually involves special training or formal education, and considered a person's lifework. It does not matter if you work sixty hours a week at General Electric, if your friends define you by the six hours you are in face.

The average person reading this column will believe they have control over the marketing of their career in drag, when actually few have the slightest clue,

To Be Continued

Continues - Page 48

Welcome to our Summer Edition of DRAG411's DRAG World, aka *Spotlight Today.*

I am overwhelmed with the success of our premiere Spring edition, with over 40,000 readers! This remarkable response has put us in FIRST PLACE as a Trade Publication devoted entirely to this craft.

Without our founding contributors, this amazing feat would never have been accomplished. I take this opportunity to thank each of our columnists for their valuable contributions, and look forward to continuing our work in promoting and presenting insightful tips, information, and humor to our readers.

On behalf of DRAG411.com, I would like to thank our Coordinating Editor, Darlene House, for her assistance with bringing this publication to life. It is with great sorrow, however, that we bid farewell to Darlene as she pursues other interests. All of us at BecHavn will miss her, and wish her every success, wherever her path may lead.

We welcome your input.

Happy Summer!

DRAG SLANG

"Bubbles"

What happens when you fart in your tight pantyhose.

Send us your slang of our facebook page

Guess Who?

It's the Cover girl who puts the "Massacre" into Mascara, here again with the filthy litter box scoop on the dumpster drag scene. I hope you all missed me since my last column, because I need loyal readers like yourself who are "Desperately Seeking Dumpster Divinity"!

Boys and Goyls, I have some raunchy, fabulous things to share with you. I consider anyone who pushes the boundaries of good taste to be A-OK in my drag handbook. To be able to stop a train with your drop dead gorgeous good looks, and de-rail it from the tracks, is "Dumpster Drag."

Do you remember being a teenager? You still may be one. We used to rent ninety-nine cent "VHS Tapes" from the local video store down the alley. My favorite B films to rent were the ones by director, "John Waters." I am not talking about the newer ones, although, "Serial Mom" was my absolute fave. I am referring to the trashy ones from the 1970's era, such as "Pink Flamingos" and "Female Trouble." It was all about the glamorous, over the top actor named, "Glenn

Harris Milstead" who portrayed a character by the name of "DIVINE."

She was a crass trailer trash version of Marilyn Monroe with over two tons of fun, snuggled in her skin tight animal print gowns, complete with big hair, lavish eyeliner and eye shadows for days! I am still inspired by all the looks of this super heroine of female illusion, and you can see it in my face when I paint myself up as Dmentia Divinyl. She is definitely a drag terrorist on a mission to exterminate "Mainstream" stereotype drag bullies and focused on ruling the "Underworld of Female Impressionists."

I recommend that you see these films. They may not be readily available on Netflix, but I am sure any hipster with half a clue can point you in the right direction on where to find these films, and you can also check out the scene clips on YouTube as well. While you're at it, stomp on by and visit my channel entitled: DMENTEDINC. Being an independent film director myself, I have made parodies of these cult classics and compiled them into one insane cinematographic movie massacre entitled: "The Complete Memoirs of Dmentia," but I digress, let us get back to the meat and potatoes of my article, shall we?

Here are some basic rules to follow when applying lip liner to get that "Come over here and let me give you a blow job" look.

Continues - Page 60

We Need Your
PET
Starbuck
Lincoln
Send us a photo
of your dressed up
pet (with their name) to
spotlight@dragbooks.com
Lexie
Veronica, Strudel, Strauss & Storm

Dmented Inc.
Presents:
"Drag Diva's of Comedy"
Monday August 27, 2012
Hosted By:
"Tinsel Garland"
at
The Woodlands Inn & Resort
in the Evolution Night Club
Tickets Available Online:
www.Dmentedinc.com
$10.00 advance / $15.00 at Door
Doors open 7pm...Showtime 8pm
Guest DJ
David
Petrilla
Starring:
Pola Frost
Gia Rylie
Comchita Swallows
Eva Ladeva
Heidi Ho
Dmentia Divinyl
Pumpkin
Mia D'Amour
w/ Our Special Guest:
Carol Ann
Carol Ann
Sophie Tucker

Be a King,
not a Prince
By Chance Wise

As a performer, I pride myself on putting on a good show. Part of a good show, in my humble opinion, is bringing an original look, an original performance, and doing my best to entertain an audience.

The question I ask myself when preparing for a performance is, what would I pay to see?

Many drag performers emulate what they see in videos from the artists that make the music, which is acceptable when they put their own interpretation into the routine as well. One thing we all see that is unacceptable is a drag performer copying another performer. I have seen blatant acts of this. It is a big reason that kings/MI's do not get the respect and recognition that they deserve, understandably so as well.

I cannot respect a performer that does this. We have free reign on how we entertain an audience, for the most part. Why would anyone feel the need to copy another king? Many entertainers out there work for years to create their drag persona. They gain a following on their hard work and their own brand of drag. It is disrespectful to try and "ride coat tails" and capitalize on their personal style and creativity. That is exactly what I see happening.

I would not want to be seen as "that king" who rips anyone off. If someone tells me that something I have done resembles another king/MI, I find pictures or videos of the king and I change anything about what I do, that may be construed as copying. Out of respect to that king/MI, I will discuss it with them, and ask if they mind that I use something similar. Costuming is a huge part of performing, and it really is an important part of the actual performance on stage. Original costumes are a great way of gaining a following on the "What is he going to wear next time?" aspect.

Costuming also adds to the feel of a song and

routine. Swarovskis add sparkle and wow factor, used by many entertainers, both male and female. Others rely on complete costumes made to specification for a number. It makes up the total package of on stage persona. There is really no limit on how we can dazzle an audience with costuming, as long as we stay within legal limits as far as nudity laws, indecency regulations, etc.

Copying a performer's costumes is not just disrespectful; it is boring for an audience. Especially, when it is done in a town or a venue that the king/MI you are copying performs on a regular basis.

There are many performers and artists out there I see that advertise, including myself, happy and willing to help kings/MI's make original costumes that are for just them. Do not be afraid to ask for help if you do not think, you are creative enough to make costumes, or do not have the artistic talent

Path to Music Etiquette
Chance Wise

to make something. It is not something that you can help, but there is help out there. It's up to you to ask for it.

"Signature" songs are a touchy subject with Male Illusionists. We all have that one song that we just click with and do better than any other song, known as a "bank" song. We do not own these songs, and all are equally available to each entertainer. It is out of respect that we ask someone to do their "signature" song. In doing another performer's "signature" song, make sure you make it yours and do it how you see it, not how they perform it.

The performer, 6 Pac said it best, "To be seen as equal, you have to bring an equal performance." I listened to 6. I tell anyone who asks for my advice on performing that it all comes down to this:

There is no set limit on what kings/MI's can do. The music is out there, and on our side right now.

Because, I think a majority of female music is a bit boring and repetitive. There is no limit on what we can do with costuming; Beer bottle tops, shirts made from bandanas, why not? Play with the outrageous and find your niche. But, find your own niche! Drag fans look for originality, they look for the most outrageous and creative performers to follow. The fans will respect you more, your peers will respect you more, and those who talk down about Male Illusionists will have no choice but to respect you. Ask for the help if you need it, because there are so many seasoned kings/MI's that WANT to help and want to see the art of Male Illusion grow and flourish.

Duct Tape Fixes Everything!

Have you ever heard the expression "Duct tape fixes everything?" Well in the wonderful world of drag, it really does. For both Male and Female Illusionists, duct tape is golden and very necessary. Newcomers have asked me the ever so popular question, "Do I have to use duct tape? Can't I just use ace bandages or a regular ole binder?" So, I have decided to dedicate this whole article on that particular subject... I speak only from my own experience and from what I was taught.

Do we have to use duct tape?

The truth of the matter is although there are some Male Illusionists that have been successful using just binders and yes, some still use ace bandages, I have found it is more convincing to hide the "girls" if you tape them down. I joke about how by the time I'm done taping, my nipples are resting under my arm pits, but realistically, it's the truth. Using the taping method allows you to conceal your breasts more effectively.

Although not in all cases, but more so for us big-breasted individuals, we simply "compress" them down against the chest therefore they look like flattened lumps. Taping allows you to completely move the babies out of the way and give the impression of having man pecs. Do not get me wrong, I do use a binder on a regular basis; I wear it over my tape. It gives support, prevents those occasional "tape popping" mishaps, and polishes the illusion.

The same thing goes for using an ace bandage, it just compresses the girls, it doesn't conceal them. Taping comes in very handy when you want to do a number with an open shirt as well. It allows you the freedom to play with your looks.

Is all Duct tape the same?

No!

There are many different brands of Duct tape, some better than others.

I personally hate the thin cheap grey stuff, it tears, it does not stick, nor does it hold well at all! Again, it may work for small-breasted individuals, but for those of us who have to use more than a few strips, it bites! My preferred brand is the authentic original "Duct Tape." This comes in many colors, it's thick and strong enough to get the job done, it doesn't cut you when you take it off, and when performing, you don't even know it's there.

When traveling out of town and performing constantly, I have been known to use Gorilla tape. To all newbie's I do NOT recommend you use this particular kind of Duct tape because it is the strongest and thickest of all duct tape, and unless your skin is conditioned to the taping process, it WILL cut and do damage to your virgin skin. Binding the boobies is NOT on a normal list of things to use Duct tape for, and your skin must get used to it. The adhesive on Gorilla tape is stronger than regular tape and unless you know what you are doing, your skin will come off with it when you remove it.

I had to learn that the hard way after performing out in the Arizona sun for a week being bound from eleven in the morning till one the following morning, By the fourth day of me being out there, poor Gunner Gatlyn looked at me with sadness in his eyes and said,

"Dude, I don't even want to tape you."

skin must get used to it. The adhesive on Gorilla tape is stronger than regular tape and unless you know what you are doing; your skin will come off with it when you remove it.

I had to learn that the hard way after performing out in the Arizona sun for a week being bound from eleven in the morning till one the following morning, By the fourth day of me being out there, poor Gunner Gatlyn looked at me with sadness in his eyes and said,

"Dude, I don't even want to tape you."

He was putting more Gorilla tape over open wound. Of course, I made him do it any way. By the time I got home, I had no skin left on my boobs. I had

to apply Aquaphor three times a day and walk around topless for a week in order to heal. Do not suggest it to anyone. (Aquaphor, by the way, is some amazing stuff when it comes to scrapes, tears, and cuts!

You can get it at any pharmacy or Wal-Mart). For those who can and do use Gorilla tape, my only advice is that you do not stay in it for more than an hour or so at a time.

Removing your tape:

There are those individuals who simply white knuckle it and rip the tape off...Bad business! By doing that, you are taking the chance of ripping your skin to shreds and scarring!

1.   WD~40 can be your best friend when removing duct tape. Spray it on, wait five minutes, and remove. It will save you the agony of tearing your skin and causing yourself much pain. This is the most painless and the easiest way. There are some other methods for those who do not like the smell of WD~40.

2.   Wait until you get home, hop in a hot shower, and remove the tape inch by inch.

3.   When removing the tape and you get to your underarm area, be careful because it is a sensitive area, and where you are most likely to be cut.

4.   When I started performing in drag, nobody warned me that removing the tape itches. If you are like me, and react to the glue on the tape, it can feel like fire ants are biting you once you remove the tape. I have tried several different kinds of tape to avoid this feeling, but it is always the same thing. I have figured out a way to correct

that problem. Make Gold Bonds Medicated powder your best friend! They come in travel size so you can tuck one in your drag box. Cover the area you taped in the powder. It not only cools your skin, it takes away the itch and discomfort.

5.   How do you keep your tape from popping? It happens at least once to the best of us...LOL, especially if you are performing a high-energy number and sweating like a pig! That is one of the reasons I use a binder over my tape, but there is another way...Elmer's Spray Adhesive! When you're done taping, tear off a few smaller strips of your tape, spray them with Elmer's and place them long ways over the edges of the tape on your chest area.

6.   How do you bind yourself? Good thing to know when you are in a situation where there is no experienced person there to help you. It takes practice, practice, practice. I used to watch Gage all the time in amazement.

When I started to travel without my wife, who

could not always go with me to bind me, I decided it was time I learned. Of course, by the time I decided to learn this particular craft, Gage had moved. There was nobody where I live to learn from, so I started out doing it by memory of what I had seen. That did not work. I looked like I had elephantiasis in the breast area. True story. I got on the phone with Gage and got tips. Then it was up to me. With much practice at home, I have now gotten to the point where I can bind myself just as tight (if not tighter) than someone who bound me. My illusion is intact and I am comfortable getting on the stage without worrying. It's not really a method that can be taught via article, text messages, or by phone, but I'll give it a try.

Here is how it is done:

1.   Use smaller strips, maybe about 6 to 8 inches long

2. Start in the center of your breast.

Apply tape while pushing breast muscle to the side.

3. Apply the same size strips to the bottom area

4. Top of the breast area will now be bulging…don't panic! Take your strip of tape and tape downward

5. Continue this process until you have gotten your boobies out of the way, and have achieved a male like appearance. Finish off with good ole' Mr. Elmer's. Your back area will be open since unless you are a contortionist, your arms will not reach that far. You can easily have someone in the dressing room slap on a few extra strips of tape across your back for added support.

Learning how to tape yourself from simply reading an article must seem completely out of left field, but once you start to play with it, you'll get the idea. The more you practice, the easier it will get. I suggest you practice at home until you have it down to a science. Good luck!

I hope I have been informative! Until next time.

summer and the weather starts to get warmer, I have noticed that people generally tend to respond in one of two ways: either joining the masses and enjoying the weather, or staying to oneself and only interacting socially when absolutely necessary. Being an outward person, I tend to get out and enjoy the beach, pool parties, yard work, etc. However, there have been times, when I have lacked motivation, or just simply felt "stuck in place," and found it difficult to shake off feelings of unworthiness.

When I find myself facing this dilemma, I have discovered that the following coping strategies often help to restore my energy, stamina, motivation, and ultimately my self-confidence:

1. Exercising: Exercise is a great way to boost one's energy, feelings of vitality, and overall health. Exercising can also be a less intimidating way to get involved with summer group activities. Such activities may include LGBT or other recreational group sporting leagues, group fitness classes, partnered trips to the gym,

Bowling leagues, neighborhood jogging or cycling activities. Often, a reason for not wanting to participate in "summer life" activities is the dissatisfaction with one's physique or level of fitness. By increasing participation in exercise, and ultimately reshaping one's body, outward appearance often improves, fitness or weight goals are achieved (or nearly achieved), and overall, one's sense of self-confidence and self-worth are strengthened, if not restored.

2. Volunteering: Volunteerism is another great way to get involved and get "outside of oneself" and to lessen feelings of depression or unworthiness. Summer time is a great time of the year to get involved with groups such as "Habitat for Humanity", "Good Will", "The United Way", "Volunteers for America", "The American Cancer Society", etc. When I have helped to feed the hungry, house the homeless, or walk with or read to the elderly, I always feel better about the good in myself, in my life.

Ultimately, understanding that I have the ability to make a difference in the world with the use of my talents and efforts are great boosts to my confidence and self-esteem.

3.   Spiritual Program/Rituals: Without endorsing any specific spiritual or religious practices, frequent prayer, mediation, spiritual fellowship, group nature walks, etc. are also healthy routines to embrace regularly, and have been shown to have powerful & positive impacts on one's mindset when one's faith or confidence in life or self is diminished.

4. Productivity: Working, producing a final product, professional collaboration, and meeting important deadlines are also effective avenues for one to not only express oneself, but to also gain feelings of satisfaction, usefulness, capability, & belief or confidence in oneself.

5. Performing: Participating in dance, drama, music, live stage, or some other performance forum, are also healthy and fun ways to boost one's confidence as well as enhance one's self-esteem.

6. Counseling: Participating in individual or group therapy (counseling) sessions often allow individuals to uncover and healthily address issues that impede or negatively impact one's self-esteem, sense of self-worth, and other barriers to positive personal and inter-personal growth.

7. Affirmation: Statements such as: "I am worthy", "I am loved", "I am well", "I am strong", "I am confident", etc. are also effective statements to make daily and have been shown to positively change an individual's perception of him or herself.

These are just a few of the many ways that one can begin to overcome mental and physical stagnation and move forward. No matter what activity or activities one might choose to become involved with, do so with consistency and enthusiasm.

Periods of seasonal transition often bring about feelings of resistance to adjust to the environmental and social changes in the world around us. The LGBT community in particular is known for hosting lavish, decadent, and ceremonious events and gatherings, especially in the summer or warmer months, but there are often many who are left in the shadows. By establishing a routine and doing so with a core or special interest group can make getting involved in summer social events, or even weekend outings, a lot less intimidating. So put your BEST foot forward this summer. Confidently embrace the beauty and strength that you have now and enjoy the warm, sunny, and breezy days ahead!

-Kevin B. Reed, MPH

All of these systems and title holders, but most of do not really know them? These interviews of four new National titleholders in the North America International system include J Estellado Knight, Sebastian Armonte, Lindsay Paige, and Asiannah B.

Mr. Gay North America International MI 2012
J Estellado Knight

What did it mean to win?
Winning for me meant a lot. First, it is, was, and has been, a great honor to be recognized for my hard work and dedication. It also means I am taking a step in the right direction as a performer. With each and every year, I want to be able to grow and also teach.

Who is your role model?
My role model outside of J mode is my grandmother, the late Margaret Jackson. She always inspired me to be all I can, and she always told me the only way to fail is not to try. J has different role models (lol). I believe my grandmother watches over Jaime and J. J has many role models, but one of the greatest, and most influential, would have to be Michael

Jackson. I strive to be the entertainer he once was.

Why the North America International Pageant system?

One of the things that got me interested in the NAI would have to be the promoters. I have worked with Andy Lewis and Aaron Hurley in the past, and it was a great experience.

What are your plans for the year of your reign?

My plans include (fingers crossed) getting the MI's to be recognized on the same platform as drag queens. People have a misconception that the bois do not have to work as hard. We as bois are more than a baseball cap and jeans.

What other titles do you held?

The only other title I hold is Mister US of A GQ 1st Alt 2011.

What advice do you give to those competing in the NAI system?

Believe in yourself. I have found that I am my biggest critic. If you exude confidence in what you are "selling," people will believe it and start to "buy" it.

What is your nonprofit platform and why did you choose it?

The nonprofit I chose was the Pituitary Awareness Network (PNA). I chose that because I have a pituitary tumor. I was diagnosed six years ago. Prior to that, I had never heard of it. I feel it is something that needs to be brought to people's attention. If caught soon enough it can be prevented/cured.

How long have you been performing?

The birth of J Estellado Knight was May 15, 2010.

Where are you from?

Born and raised in good ole Springfield, Illinois.

Continues - Page 68

In the drag world, you learn to expect the unexpected. Murphy 's Law almost always applies in that whatever can go wrong, will go wrong. This is including, but not limited to, costume malfunctions, music malfunctions, prop malfunctions and makeup faux pas. While these things are bound to happen, you also learn to roll with the punches. I've seen many a hissy fit thrown over music not working, or stopping, or a costume not doing what it should be doing, and to me it's just laughable, especially at a bar show. What kills me, are the folks who experience a mishap and expect the entire show to come grinding to a halt while they attempt to fix it.

People... it's DRAG.

Find your sense of humor, improvise, and move on.

I've learned to laugh at all the missteps that have happened throughout my drag career, and some of them have been doozies! Like the time I went to put a pair of pants on for a show and they literally fell apart at the seams. No. Really. I had to duct tape them back together and pray that they would last the 3 minutes I needed them to.

just one piece of tape here, one piece of tape there, both my pant legs were taped from the waistband to the floor, on both the inner and outer seams. The crotch seam had to be taped from the front button, down and around to the back belt loop.

Oh yeah, THAT was sexy, let me tell you!

I was terrified that the tape would not hold, or the pants would find another place to fall apart and I would end up on stage in my drawers. No one wants to see that. Luckily, they held… for that one number and that was it.

I have had music stop numerous times at shows; on CDs that had been tested to be sure, they worked. Generally, no big deal, until it happens at a pageant. What a clusterf*ck that was. Talent portion of competition. CD had worked fine in rehearsal earlier in the day. Thirty-seconds in: *blip*. No more music, but we kept going. I was with four backup dancers, and we had the crowd on their feet, clapping

and cheering and we never missed a beat, but my god, it was nerve wracking! To add insult to injury, I was accused of staging the stunt on purpose, to gain the sympathy vote.

Bitch, please!

If I wanted to go for the sympathy vote, I would perform on crutches or something. You know… I am sneaky like that. I managed to slip a note to the DJ, telling him to cut the music thirty seconds into my talent. Even today, I roll my eyes. Listen… hear them rolling.

I have seen queens come untucked, kings come unbound; neither is pretty. If you have never been privy to a king's binding coming undone, count yourself lucky. Imagine a king, with a decent sized chest, up on stage, open shirt, rocking out, then POP! It is a boobie! If you are lucky, the king notices and attempts to hide it behind an arm or a shirt, but it happens without being noticed. Suddenly you have an entertainer kicking Nickelback's ass with a pendulous breasticle blowing in the breeze. Most kings learn to laugh this off, which is what you absolutely must do!

Throwing fits and beating yourself up over something like this accomplishes nothing. I mean, you had the best of intentions and did not mean to come undone on purpose... at least I hope not.

It could be worse. You could have packed your costumes for a show, not even thinking about the fact that you have not worn at least one of these costumes for several months. In your oversight, you become delusional and assume that you are the same size you were several months ago. If you are anything like me, that is a bunch of crap. In my head, I am still the fifty pounds less that I am now. It is an idea quickly stomped into the ground the second I

try to squeeze myself into a pair of pants without the benefit of silicone lube, Crisco or lard to help with the squeezing.

This is when panic sets in. You have no other outfit except for the shorts and t-shirt you came in. You HAVE to get into these pants! Meanwhile, everyone in the dressing room is giving you odd looks watching you try to wiggle surreptitiously your way into pants that are a good four sizes too small. Shit, if the chicks at the mall can do it, so can I! You try to suck in your belly, lay across a pool table, or the floor, as you maneuver the pants up over your thighs. Yes! They are on!

Almost!

How the hell do I button these damn things? Seriously, how can you NOT laugh at things like this? It is comedy at its finest. God forbid there was a microphone and a video camera backstage at a show.

One more snafu for you. In the end, it's just drag and if you lose your sense of humor about it, you may as well pack up and go home. Take yourself too seriously, and in the end, no one wants to be around you because no one wants a Debbie Downer around.

While in Modesto last year, I decided to do something different and tape. Why I decided to do this, I do not know. I still do not know. I must have been drunk or something. Regardless, I taped rather than using my tried and true binder. It was a gorgeous day, sunny with a breeze. Gunner and I had a half hour set, so we alternated numbers: him, me, him, etc. It went great.

The crowd dug us. Did I mention it was 82 and breezy?

Guess who overheated?

Yep, this ginger king. I ended up stumbling over to the tent, vomiting all over the place and then sitting on the grass, unbound, trying to keep my

Russian Figure Skater's Wardrobe Malfunction

boobs from falling out of my shirt, while a gay prison nurse (yes, really) put wet paper towels on the back of my neck, my ankles and my armpits, and fed me fruit. Not embarrassing in the least. I mean, seriously. Who does that? I managed to throw up once more on the way to the car, but we laughed about it.

This the moral to my fable. Whether your pants are falling off, your bits and pieces decide to come untucked, your music goes on vacation, or you end up sitting on the ground being fed grapes by a gay prison nurse, remember to keep your sense of humor. After all, it is just drag and life is too short to take yourself too seriously.

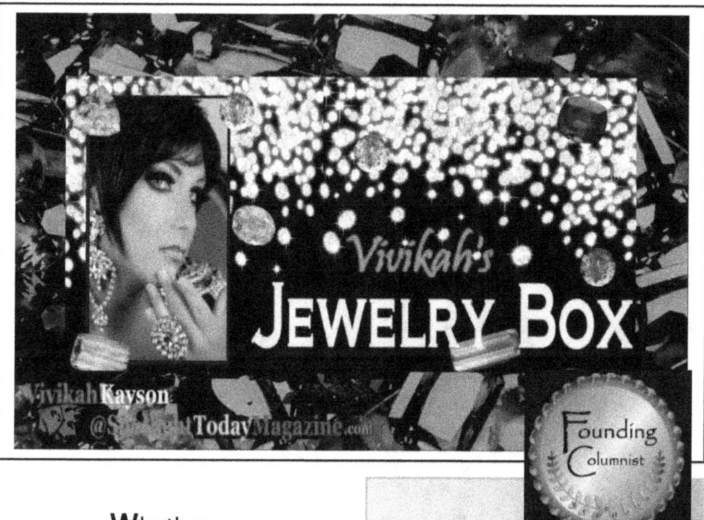

Whether you are a female illusionist, transsexual or a biological woman, one thing that we will always have in common is our love for jewelry. It is understood, bigger is better! The more bling you can add to your already fabulous outfit is just as important as deciding what foundation and eye shadow you will apply.

Of course, size really does matter when you are picking out the perfect jewelry set to match that sexy outfit for a night on the town or for more of a subdued look heading up the corporate office meeting.

Let us discuss the earrings. Not only do you need to pick the accenting colors to match your outfit, but also you have to consider the plans on wearing your hair, design of your dress etc. If you are going for a more professional business presence, then you are not going to want to wear the large ear rings that you would expect to see on Friday night on stage during a show. If you have, your hair pulled up into a bun, use smaller to mid-size earrings. Although, when going for that stunning WOW factor, then larger is always better.

Your necklace needs to be coordinated to the style and cut of the outfit you plan on wearing. For example, if you have a dress that has a plunging chest but wraps around the neck, then a necklace may not be needed. If you feel that you are still looking for the attention factor, then keep it simple with this style of dress. Too large, or wraps, will take away from the sexy design.

Of course, the ring should never be skimped on. Whether you are a female illusionist or everyday woman, we all use our hands to speak what we need not to say. Therefore, start out any conversation showing your audience that not just anything will do. Only the finest Diamond – Emerald etc. is for you. Whether you are standing in line at your local coffee hut, or at the bar of your favorite club, everyone is checking out your hands to see if there is a ring, therefore make it count.

There are many options out there. You have everything from diamonds, my personal favorite, to various knock off-lookalikes. No matter what you choose to wear, make sure that it tells the story of whom you are. Make sure the color of your fab outfit matches the color and design of your jewelry. If you are wearing colored stones, AB or clear, this can change the look.

Knock them dead! Show them that cheap is not a word of your vocabulary. Whether you are a female illusionist, transsexual or biological female, the one thing that unites us is our love for jewelry. Embrace it, go ahead, and demand nothing but the best, after all you deserve it.

Marilyn Monroe had it right "Diamonds are a girl's best friend."

Legislative information from the United States and around the world. If you have questions about any of this legislation, please contact me.

London, England

Liberal Democrat Lynne Featherstone will today unveil plans to legislate to bring in gay marriage before 2015. Vowing to be a personal *champion for gay rights*, Miss Featherstone will risk controversy by arguing that the Coalition should go even

further in the future. At present, gays and lesbians can enter civil partnerships, which offer most of the legal protections of marriage, but the term *marriage* is not used. The Equalities Minister will also announce that Britain should be a 'world leader for gay rights'. For whom the bells toll: David Cameron is backing legislation to legislate gay marriage. The coalition is to push ahead with plans for gay marriage following the personal intervention of David Cameron.

Read more:
http://www.dailymail.co.uk/news/article-2038427/Gay-marriage-legal-Britain-2015.html#ixzz1xZsjUdMz

Legal Sex Change

You must present a court-ordered name change and a letter from a surgeon indicating that you have completed Sex Reassignment Surgery (SRS) in order to change your name and sex on Federal documents such as Social Security cards and passports. Some people have been successful at acquiring passports with name and sex changes without completing SRS surgery, but it is difficult. If attempting to get your gender marker changed under your state's law, it is important to know what your state's law. One of the easiest ways to learn about the State's requirements is to call the entity that issues driver's licenses.
Read more:
http://www.tsroadmap.com/reality/passport.html

San Francisco, California

Transgender Law Center applauds the U.S. Department of Justice (DOJ) today for releasing long-awaited new standards mandated by the Prison Rape Elimination Act (PREA) of 2003. Today's federal regulations, which include important guidelines about the housing and treatment of transgender inmates, mark the first time the U.S. Government has created national standards to address the prevalence of sexual assault in prisons, jails, juvenile detention facilities throughout the country. President Obama released a concurrent memorandum directing "all agencies with Federal confinement facilities that are not already subject to the Department of Justice's final rule to work with the Attorney General to propose any rules or procedures necessary to satisfy the requirements of PREA." This will apply to immigration detention facilities run by the Department of Homeland Security, among other agencies.

Read more:
http://transgenderlawcenter.org/cms/blogs/552-26

Washington, DC

Gay rights activists have made significant strides in recent years on marriage and military service, but one long-standing policy goal remains elusive: a federal law to ban discrimination against gay workers. Gays now can serve openly in the military. Gay couples now have some form of legal recognition in nineteen states and the District of Columbia. However, in 29 states, gay workers can still be fired or denied promotions simply because they are gay.

Read more:
http://www.kansascity.com/2012/06/11/3652764/federal-ban-on-job-bias-still.html#storylink=cpy

Missouri

Republican lawmakers in Missouri are defending their controversial bill to ban the teaching of sexual orientation in schools as a way to prevent students from learning about the "homosexual agenda," the "heterosexual agenda" and bestiality. A group of 20 Republican state representatives introduced the so-called "don't say gay" bill last week to prevent the teaching of sexual orientation in public schools, with the exception of classes relating to human reproduction. The group includes some of the most powerful Republicans in the Missouri legislature -- House Speaker Steve Tilley (R-Perryville), Majority Leader Tim Jones (R-Eureka) and the chairs of the Rules and the Ways and Means committees. Tennessee legislators have been debating a similar proposal.

Darby v. Orr
Case representing same-sex couples in Illinois seeking to marry.

People v. Plunkett
Case involving a man who bit a police officer and whose saliva was ruled a "dangerous instrument" because he has HIV.

Lopez Berera v. Holder
Amicus brief to the U.S. Court of Appeal for the Ninth Circuit in support of asylum protection for Karolina Lopez Berera, a transgender Mexican woman living with HIV.

In re Warm Sands Cases
Amicus brief with the Appellate Division of the Superior Court of Riverside County asking the court to reverse several convictions from an anti-gay sting operation in the Warm Sands neighborhood of Palm Springs.

Sevcik v. Sandoval
Lawsuit filed in the U.S. District Court for the District of Nevada arguing that Nevada's ban on marriage equality violates the Equal Protection Clause of the Constitution.

Couch v.
Wayne Local School District
Maverick Couch is a high school junior threatened with suspension if he wore a T-shirt bearing the message "Jesus Is Not a Homophobe."

Cervelli v. Aloha B&B
Case representing a lesbian couple denied accommodation at a Hawaii commercial business establishment.

Arizona v.
United States
Amicus brief to the Supreme Court of the United States supporting an injunction against provisions of Arizona SB 1070.

Buntemeyer v.
Iowa Dept. of
Public Health
Lambda Legal case in which a legally married same-sex couple in Iowa gave birth to a stillborn baby and was issued a death certificate by the Iowa Department of Public Health with one of the mother's names removed with correction fluid.

Dept. of HHS
v. Florida
US Supreme Court case challenging the constitutionality of Affordable Care Act, a law that expands access to health insurance for millions of Americans, including those living with HIV.

Keeton v. Anderson-Wiley
Case in which a counseling student sues her school for requiring a remediation plan that included greater exposure to LGBT patients.

Cervelli v. Aloha B&B
Case representing a lesbian couple denied accommodation at a Hawaii commercial business establishment.

Send in your wildest pair of shoes.
You must send in a Close-up photo of you wearing them!

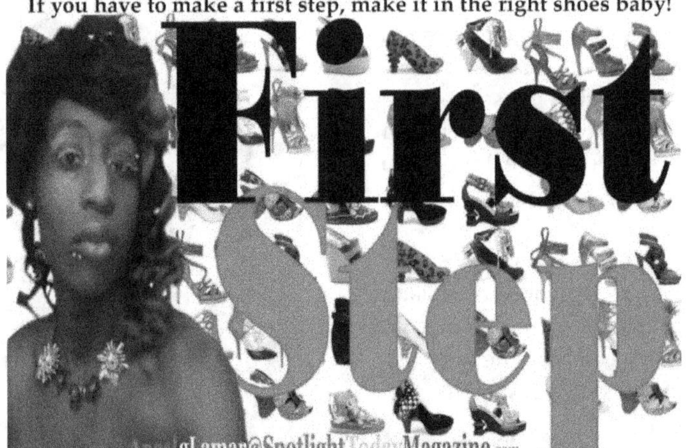

The New Queen on the Block

I thought about "How hard it is being an entertainer," at my last performance.

It is hard to be "the new performer" in a show bar filled with strangers. You have to network to find new venues to perform. You must cultivate and create your own fan base. It is hard, and the queens at the bars do not make it any easier. I guess I forgot how it was. It took me showing up in Iowa, and hitting the bars often to locate queens that liked me.

Now here I am again, in a new town called Tampa, with new venues, new talented queens, and new possibilities to discover new fans.

Last time I went bar hopping, and stumbled upon an amateur night at a local national chain. My friends were pushing me to enter. I felt out of place, shy, unprepared, and I had only performed once since my arrival. I went to the DJ, wearing only a pair of number thirty-three eyelashes, makeup, and heels and registered my name for the competition. Without practicing, without a wig or an outfit, I lip-synced my ass off to win. I thought the other queens in the bar would cheer me as a new girl (and the only drag queen in the final countdown of the competition); to show me support for attempting to get on stage without notice. I expected their understanding, since they knew what it took to stand on stage unprepared. This did not happen. Not a single one cheered or clapped for me (even though I won). I wouldn't have won if I was bad. It caught me off guard in my new town, as I discovered a couple of them kicking me down to the crowd.

The vision of the movie *Mean Girls* played in my mind.

I once again had the feeling of being pushed away as the new girl, for no other reason than I was once again in my new home... the new queen on the block. There are queens wanting to learn the craft, to learn what is going on, and how to get themselves out there. However, most do not get a break. I understand if you do not pay your dues, you should not be headlining. The new girls are not begging for a star on their dressing room door in the beginning, but a fighting chance.

Today I write to ask all of you to help show them the way. Instead of trash talking about them, be the light of wisdom and insight; be the leader, the wise one in the room. Be the good Samaritan in the drag room often filled with bitterness. Say, "I may not teach you all my tricks, but I will tell you the basics to get you started." It will make a difference in someone's life.

I miss this from Iowa, but not every town is Cedar Rapids. Most of you live in areas that are not Iowa. They held the new girls' hand long after they taught her a new skill. The girls out there gave you the confidence to fly solo, but provided her with the security of feeling she was part of a family.

Do not make this another Nicki Minaj and Lil'Kim feud. Do you remember when you were in high school, when some kid moved to your town in the

middle of the school year?

Remember the first time you did drag? Take that memory to help build someone's life from your life experience. I promise; you have the chance to develop a better, more positive drag world, one new queen at a time.

Alexis De La Mer sent in this photo of Kamden Cass, her, Sherry Vine, and Madisyn Michaels at The Flamingo Resort in St. Petersburg, Florida. PHOTO: Jack Butera.   Send us your group photos.

To pageant or not to pageant

Decide to write an editorial worth reading. I did not want to write about crafts or wigs just because that is something I am familiar with. I decided to write about a subject matter that could be offensive to those that love to compete in small or bar pageants. This is just my opinion and not DRAG World's. Not all competitions are this way, or do business in this manner. I have been in four pageants and will leave out the names for the sake of tarnishing a name

In my very first competition, there were only three of us competing. I did my own face and hair. The winning queen had someone else do her face and was wearing someone else's hair and costumes, nothing was hers. I just thought to myself that I really would not want to win a crown if nothing I did was actually the reason I won. I took my first alternate position with pride, because I knew I did everything myself, and I earned it. On my second try, in the same system with the same promoter, I decided to do take the path of the previous winner. I had someone do my face and hair and dressed me in their clothes. I once again won first alternate.

I hated everything about

how I looked; it was not me. I tried a new system for my next pageant. I can say that the queen that won did great. I did think that the two queens that won were both part of the same bar, and that owner was the promoter for this three-crowned event. Not too long after, I was in a show promoting the first system I was in, doing my first alternate obligation. I happened to overhear a conversation between an assistant of the promoter and a former titleholder. The assistant was asking the titleholder to do a step down event in the near future. The titleholder was upset. She began explaining her disappointment in discovering she won her crown because the promoter of the system wanted her to win, regardless of judges and points, and she did not feel right doing a step down.

I began to ask questions. Several queens stated that, depending on the

system and the promoter, you could even buy yourself a win. It made me sick to my stomach because of the amount of time and money you invest in these competitions. I entered my last pageant because I was asked, and for the sake of giving it one more chance. I entered a creative competition in this pageant. You had a creative eveningwear judged portion. I created an evening gown made of syringes, covered it completely and then covered it in stones. My gown's theme was drugs and HIV prevention. I really wanted to know who was in this pageant, so I asked, but they would not tell me. I wanted to know who the judges were, but they would not tell me. I believe I was just a filler.

That night, out of the five of us in the pageant, three of us created our gowns. The National winner was there and asked me to go in back with her. She told me if I do not win or at least get first alternate for my gown creation, that this competition had its winners already. It made me think of the conversation I had overheard, since this was the same owner, just a different system.

As I expected, I only won the spirit award, which to me was just a "thank you for spending hundreds of dollars and being a filling a slot" award. The queens that won both spots wore bought gowns and were not even memorable. I decided not to pursue another crown. I could easily buy my own crown and still keep the way I felt about myself intact. Every judge gave me every point for my gown and wrote that my gown was the most creative of the evening. The store bought gown won the category. It made no sense that I did not win that category. I guess they wanted it to look like a clean sweep that she won every category. I understand that other systems are legit, but this is just my opinion, and the way Makanoe C's It.

Continued from Page 11

as most confuse promotions with marketing, talent with marketing, and a host of other incorrect observations of them explaining, "they understand their art." This is the second mistake. Marketing is not about art. Marketing is a science. A big difference, which explains the confusion, I hope to dispel in this cover story.

Andy Warhol is an artist. What made him famous was his natural ability to create a massive market for his unique interpretation of his craft (and the world around him).

He created his market, then sold his merchandise, his art inside of the market he created.

Why would you want to compete for attention as an impersonator repeating the same steps as five thousand other performers? If you are a dime a dozen, you will be paid accordingly.

Now do not get me wrong, drag marketing has nothing to do with your ability to do drag. This article has nothing to do with your performance on stage. The content of Drag Marketing has everything to do with the image of you, that you decide to project. I began college for theatrical arts before transferring to economics, a better feeling major for my talents. I decided not to pursue the stage after discovering the craft hinged heavily on luck over skills.

The top hundred actors were "not the best actors" in their craft. Their success and money rarely correlated with their skills as an actor. I called it the Hamburger Effect. No company on earth earns more money on hamburgers than McDonald's. Few people on earth vote McDonalds as the best hamburger they ever ate in their entire life. Marketing.

How many times do you see a performer that is A HAMBURGER; their popularity is much larger than their talent?

Marketing is using science to create a strategic path to place you in the right location at the right time, in the best format to accomplish the goals set within a designated deadline. Using these eight steps will get you closer to accomplishing them, and just like any digital version of *Spotlight Today* Magazine; the paper version is available: www.SpotlightTodayMagazine. com.

**A Rose By Any Other Name
Is Not A Rose**

Stop using a name that sounds like fifty other performers. Go on facebook (our host, so I tend to use their name continuously since you are able to promote yourself free to an audience of nine-hundred million people using these steps). Type in the name you plan to use. Check out the other performers using your name. Are you as clever as you thought you were, or did another performer start making steps next to your path? Worse yet, did a slew of performers use knock off names in the same direction?

.2.

Harness The Internet

Go to Network Solutions www.NetworkSolutions.com (or any other internet provider). Type your stage name to examine extensions available to purchase. It will offer for ten bucks the option to acquire it as a dot com (.com) or a litany of other options including com, net, co, org, mobi, info, biz, tel, eu, co.uk, de, us, us.com, pro, asia, and the highly restricted xxx. Dot com is the most popular, but has nothing to do with search engine rankings. For those of you under the impression that rankings implies if you are a booger or diva… we need to talk. Rankings is your placement from the top page of the search results on Google, Bing (note Bing now powers Yahoo), and a host of hundreds of search engines around the world. All of our projects are on page one (and often smother the first thousand postings in each category).

DragBooks.com has the same value as someone purchasing the web address DragBooks.net.   Even something as bizarre as DragBooks.de would have the same ability to overtake the .com address. The address does not determine the placement, so do not be intimidated to purchase an extension not often used, to have it attached to your stage name. The value is not in the address, but the site you create on your hosting package.

You can obtain your address and each extension for three to ten dollars for the first year (total). I do not recommend this option, as all it does is lock down the address and offers you nothing to create the site. An address is not your hosting package. I suggest you call Network Solutions (the oldest hosting company) and discuss purchasing a small-Unix hosting package. The first year set up will only be around a hundred bucks for the hosting, without you having to also pay for the address, includes the option to add multiple email accounts directing traffic to you (with your own email system for each of those addresses), and is extremely easy to set up and use instantly. You will create a presence around the world within hours. I constantly assist people setting up their accounts in return for lunch. Every time a person leaves my home after a tutoring session, they are amazed on the simplicity of creating an international marker.

Note: Do not add anything clever to your stage name, other than your stage name. I will explain later.

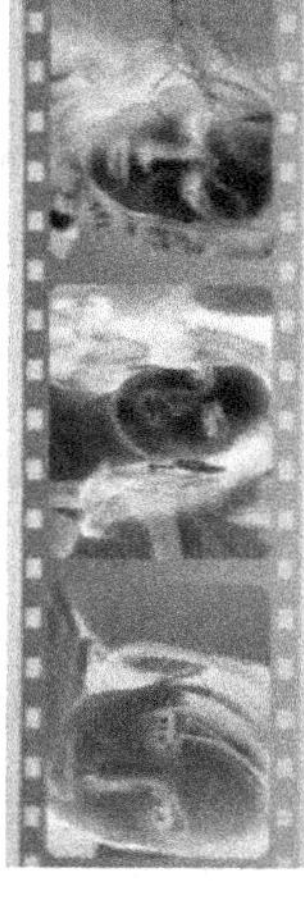

.3.
Control Your Image

This is not 1984.

You are not leaving Kmart with an envelope of crappy photos and rows of brown negatives, forced to purchase alongside toilet paper and Glidden paint. We live in a digital world where insufficient photographs vanish at the flick of the dial and Photoshop corrects errors once relegated to future generations of laughter.

Get in the habit of asking for two photos clicked each time someone decides they need to capture you on film. This allows you the option to select the photo that best meets your needs to post in your album. Do not feel you have to keep an unwanted tag of some crappy photo on your facebook wall.

Right click your mouse to steal the great photographs taken by other people.

Learn to use your damn camera, so when you hand it to a friend they have the correct settings. All those numbers on the screen have a purpose. Each one can define your image to a millimeter of perfection. Only one out of ten camera owners have the slightest idea of the functions offered on their own camera. This is not a good statistic for those creating an online presence one image at a time.

Stop posting uncropped photographs. If fifty percent of your picture is the back marketing yourself). Our company collects single headshots of performers to place in book and magazine projects. It is constantly a disaster with few performers having the slightest idea of how to submit a close-up face shot. If you can repeat your face area three times in the image, it is not a close-up. The word contrast means opposite of nature. Black-White. Green-Yellow. A photograph of you should be in contrast.

You should easily be identifiable in a photo. In our company, we have a term we call, "The Middlesexx," named after my dear friend Tiffani Middlesexx. During our collection of headshots for The Official Drag Handbook, she led the charge of hundreds of entertainers sending us a photo of them standing in front of a black wall, with black hair, and in a black outfit. Oh yes, and she is black. Steve Hammond and I laugh about it to this day. We concluded that performers think contrast means matching in a Garanimal print. A head shot is a front-on, facing straight at the camera photograph, with the face being the center of the picture and containing minimal or no surroundings. The facial expression is usually neutral.

High definition content of photographs and video is quickly becoming the standard, not only in this industry, but in each American household. Even a simple free format as facebook displays high def photos with incredible clarity. Take advantage of this resource as an entertainer. Instantly delete images that do not meet your new standards. Just because mom took the photo, does not qualify the photo to be in your new marketing campaign. Keep mom's photo on your personal page or screensaver. You do not see RuPaul posting faded, haphazard, off-focus, or blurred photos to her site

to represent her image to the world; you should expect nothing less from your life.

If you want to be "A-Game," you have to stop promoting yourself as if it is your Junior High School Class Yearbook. The top entertainers of today are using tools of tomorrow to polish their image. The photographs they are starting to collect are so polished, refined, and developed by professional photographers that those of you not making the time to clean up your albums will soon find their image portrayed as unskilled; which is the last image you wish to display.

The tools to step up your game are free on the internet. You just need to make time, push past apathy and the fear of technology, and you will realize the artful, creative side of you will adore playing with the images you post.

.4.
Raking

When you are sitting around bored one day, open your social media accounts and start raking your pages. Your folders, albums, postings, walls, comments, videos, photographs, and written interaction with people on your sites, ALL represent you to nine hundred million potential fans (just on facebook alone). Go through each account to tighten and organize the message represented on your page. The message is your interpretation of "How you see yourself as a performer, and conveying that message to your potential fan base."

Comb (rake) through your social networking pages removing random comments to streamline page content for easy access for your potential "

and current fans. You want them to return continuously to your site for entertainment. It is hard to be entertained in the home of a FACEBOOK HOARDER, too busy to realize that every comment, no matter how mundane and random now clutters their page like seven foot newspaper piles sitting next to the hoarder's toilet.

Think of your page as a book in school, where you went through with a yellow highlighter to earmark the most important information needed for your understanding of the subject. Use this premise to mark your social media pages by eliminating cluttered content. Not one person reading this article has more profiles and pages than I do. I understand the statement, "I don't have time."

My reply is simple, "Your image is your greatest asset when you are not physically on stage, performing. The average fan will spend more time on your site, if done properly, than they will by standing in front of you watching you shake your bon-bons. Your image bestows upon the public the best of you. It represents what you are and what you wish to be in the future. It is you reaching out to your fans to bring them into your magical world.

"Make time!"

My reply is simple, "Your image is your greatest asset when you are not physically on stage, performing. The average fan will spend more time on your site, if done properly, than they will by standing in front of you watching you shake your bon-bons. Your image bestows upon the public the best of you. It represents what you are and what you wish to be in the future. It is you reaching out to your fans to bring them into your magical world.

"Make time!"

.5.
Sign Your
John Handcock Baby!

The internet offers over one hundred free programs that allow you to add words to a photo. Dozens of cameras on the market will let you add a tag line on the photograph. If there is a club owner in Nova Scotia noticing some random photo clunking around with me standing next to Scooby Doo, I can promise you this… off in the corner, there in small print are the words, "infamoustodd.com."

You want people to instantly place in their mind,

I'll go anywhere to make you smile!

your name, likeness, and the link we discussed in the Harness the Internet chapter (section two). By having your name as the internet link in the corner, you do not have to clutter the photo twice with wording. This makes a great rule since wording distracts from the quality of the photo and creates clutter, which distracts readers. The photo now highlights both you and generates potential traffic flow to your website.

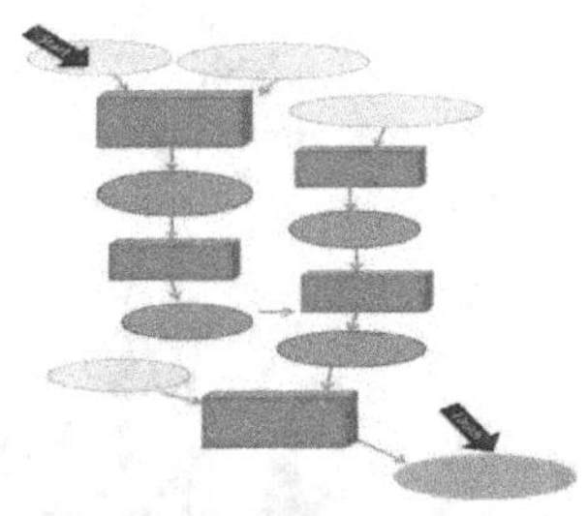

.6.
Ready For
My Close Up!

Actual close-up photos sent in. Can you explain the difficulties in each photograph? I love all these entertainers, and most will smack me in the head for showing these dozen photos. Thankfully, they are my friends. I am stunned that the majority of you have few high quality photographs of yourself, and out of the 28% that believe you do, only 2% are right.

Two percent is a very bad number. I could not picture bringing a final Exam Paper home to my mother as a child, with a large "2%" circled in red on the top of the page. A photo. The face area cannot repeat three times in a photo. Clear, not cloudy, eyes forward... Hey, I did not make up these rules. Google it.

.7.

Write, Yeah Right

Getting your name out to the public does not always mean in the form of a poster a venue spams across their websites, pages, or posts in their physical locations to talk about a show including you as a performer. You should expect nothing less from venues filling their cash registers with your talent. Not everyone hangs at a bar; including the bar owners (though as a previous bar owner, I would challenge this comment). You cannot always be on stage with your minions cowering at your feet. A photograph the audience will glance at for seconds, though I have watched many of you staring at your own photographs for hours.

Wikipedia, "Gay Publications" and you will see a host of almost a hundred magazines published around the world. You are reading a trade publication by BecHavn Publishing and Production Group. DRAG411 is the largest provider of books on the subject of impersonation, and is part of the BecHavn family. All around you are publishers begging for your wisdom to share with their readers. These readers often spend more time reading a gay paper than they do watching an entire drag show. Unlike a show, the publication is instant gratification. Unlike a show, a reader has the benefit of taking your column home to bed tonight. Expand your fan base by reaching into the community through periodicals. The payoff is extraordinarily positive for the entertainer and pays off for decades as name recognition increases in the non-bar communities.

.8.
Tag, You're It!!

Make sure photos include many people you can tag, so they will share the photographs on their end. With your new web address as your name in the corner, your fans and friends now unwittingly have become your marketing muscle. I constantly find clever statements to make into postcards uploaded onto facebook, so other people will start sharing them across facebook. Most of you have accidently shared a comment on your facebook page without realizing it was me. Wear purple for teen bullying a few years ago went viral with Brullt.com plastered in the corner. Some inspirational or motivational comments with InfamousTodd.com, a sick pair of drag shoes with DRAG411.com, the list continues with dozens of other sites generating back to my platform. NEVER USE THE WORDS www. or http://www. on the title imprinted on the photo. You do not need this prefix in a search.

Guerilla Marketing uses alternative means to create attention, using a small amount of cash. I hit over fifty million people on facebook since joining the site, without spending a dime. Where else can you find a platform for you to become exactly the performer you see in your mind? Not even a stage allows you this opportunity. Think about it, nine hundred million potential fans are going to make a determination of you based not on your stage performance, but of the image you create. Make them so overwhelmed by your talent here, and they will follow you to your venues. Thousands will become your fans; treat them with the respect they deserve and build a page worthy of them enjoying, sharing, and promoting amongst their fans.

Even if you don't keep the tag or photo by fans on your page, make a positive comment below the photos they post. It will ensure they don't take it wrong once you remove the photo. If you steal it, tell them. Most love the fact that you appreciate them. If you use their photo, credit the photo to them; it didn't cost you a penny and they will be flooding the newsfeeds with comments.

You want them to be screaming to their friends, "LOOK AT THIS ENTERTAINER, THEY ROCK," behind your back. You may get a few of them now, some of you may even have a thousand visitors a month to your page, but the percentage is against you. Those returning week after week, even less. The path to changing is constant. There are no easy answers. Those on the top are on the top because they are busting their asses to stay on top. The rules change and are fluid, but the ones I posted above are 100% successful. If you have a better plan than mine, write an article and send it in with a close up.

Yes, a close up.

performer you see in your mind? Not even a stage allows you this opportunity. Think about it, nine hundred million potential fans are going to make a determination of you based not on your stage performance, but of the image you create. Make them so overwhelmed by your talent here, and they will follow you to your venues. Thousands will become your fans; treat them with the respect they deserve and build a page worthy of them enjoying, sharing, and promoting amongst their fans.

Even if you do not keep the tag or photo by fans on your page, make a positive comment below the photos they post. It will ensure they do not take it wrong once you remove the photo. If you steal it, tell them. Most love the fact that you appreciate them. If you use their photo, credit the photo to them; it did not cost you a penny and they will be flooding the newsfeeds with comments.

You want them to be screaming to their friends, "LOOK AT THIS ENTERTAINER, THEY ROCK," behind your back. You may get a few of them now, some of you may even have a thousand visitors a month to your page, but the percentage is against you. Those returning week after week, even less. The path to changing is constant. There are no easy answers. Those on the top are on the top because they are busting their asses to stay on top. The rules change and are fluid, but the ones I posted above are 100% successful. If you have a better plan than mine, write an article and send it in with a close up.

Yes, a close up.

Continued from page 15

First, always draw on your lips with a black or dark brown eye pencil; be sure to color in the internal creases of each side just a bit to give them some 3D depth perception to your onlookers.

Next, be sure to color in your entire lips with whatever your lightest eye shadow color you are going to be using for that night. This is usually the color "white" and it will apply a secure base for the next color(s) you use as well as build your lips to look fuller.

The third, and most important, step is to be sure that whatever lip

colors you use are metallic or have gloss sheen to them, and finally hit the lower plump part of your lip with a small schmear or lips a Glamazon finish. This will make your lips look like they should be pressed against a bulbous head, and if you play your cards right, they might be before the end of the night.

Be sure to reapply this white streak on your lip makeup that comes off during this process, or if you use props in your act, where you insert things in your mouth. Your lips and eyes are your most important assets in drag make believe and you do not want to "F@*k It Up!"

Another amazing trick to dazzle your fans with in applying your face for the evening is a face-lift. I am not talking about "Cher" or even "Chad Michaels" for that matter. I mean give yourself the impression that you had the work done and spare yourself some chump change and painful needles in the process.

"Contouring," starts at the point of taking your blush color to make a deep, dark, and delicious, and very carefully apply some down the outer sides of your nose on each side. Be careful not to over apply and never on the slope of the beak. Take an index finger full of white eye shadow, or in some cases white concealer, and starting from the crease at the top between your eye sockets on your nose slope, follow with your finger straight down the center, but only to about a quarter of an inch before the end of your nose. Do not apply it completely to the tip, as it serves as an illusion. This will give you the needed "Beverly Hills Nose Job" appearance. It will conceal your identity from those who know you as a boy a lot better. This

simple application can make all the difference in your beauty, and give you a "Carpet Fresh New Look"!

Now I cannot give you the low down on all of my many makeup illusions all in one article, so you will have to return the next time for more clever hints on how to make yourself look like a drama queen.

Now let me talk to you just for a moment on the topic of "Shmegma." I hope you know what this is or means, and for those of you without a clue, here it is for you, It is the head cheese that looks and smells a bit like "Feta" that falls off the tip of an uncut prick. Although it spreads nice on a Ritz cracker if you do not have any cream cheese, due to its chunky white chalky consistency, it is better to know about this little

Continues - Page 92

Hello again readers.

In my last article, I explained how I got my start as a "Drag" entertainer. In this issue, I am going to take us all down memory lane. I have been around the gay scene for almost forty years, performing for thirty-one, and witnessed many changes.

Music is a huge part of the gay life. It is ever changing while marking periods in our lives.

Every time I hear one of the "oldies," I am immediately transported to where I was, when I first heard each song. I can remember all the old disco tunes of the late seventies. I remember the first time I heard a "new" singer called Madonna!

Over the years, we gay folk have hitched our wagon to many of the "Divas." We listened and followed Miss Ross, Bette Midler, Cher, and Tina Turner to name a few.

Today's young gays will feel the same in a few years, but with different divas of their era. I am sure Brittany and Gaga will be at the top of their list. Music has brought our community together, and at times, has been our common bond.

The "Drag Show" has long been a staple of the gay entertainment scene, but has seen sweeping changes over the years. In many clubs I worked in, shows were not commonplace. For the most part, holidays and special occasions, were the only time drag shows were done. The idea of a weekly show was rare. The drag show has evolved over the years and it is now easier to become a "Queen."

Make-up, wigs, costumes, and shoes are easily available on line. I can remember scouring the thrift stores and Goodwill trying to find something that would fit me! As the drag show became more popular, the market got flooded with newbies and wannabes, this became a double-edged sword. Many of the new kids wanted instant fame and had not paid their dues and in turn, this has really hurt the image of a professional show.

The gay club scene has had its ups and downs over the years, from being hidden in unsavory neighborhoods to becoming mainstream legitimate business's. I have fond memories of scoping a club before you entered. My friends and I would drive around the block to see if it was safe to go in!

Small neighborhood bars are dying, replaced with big dance clubs and the internet. The neighborhood bar was the place to go to meet someone or find a date, if only for the night. Over years, the internet became the place to hook-up. Now a person can stay home cruising online.

I am old school.

I always think it is better to meet someone face to face, buy them a drink, and get to know them better, so until next time kids, remember to get out there and keep it old school!

**Send us a photo of your pet dressed up.
Send us a photo of three or more performers in a group.
Don't forget to include names. Send to our facebook group.**

Victoria Silverstone, Alisa Summers, and Angel gLamar at Hamburger Mary's in Tampa, Florida.

Photo: Hector Acevedo

Reprint. Not original to STM

FAKE IT

Stage Presence

One of the things I hear from fans and other entertainers when I leave the stage is, "You have amazing stage presence." I am appreciative knowing so many people enjoy what I do as a performer. It does not come easy. In order to be a successful entertainer, you must have stage presence. Next to knowing the words to your song, it is the most important aspect of any traveling entertainer.

"But don't you have to be born with that talent," you ask?

Absolutely not!

You can FAKE IT, but never assume you can quickly master it. It is going to take time, and plenty of practice. You can do it. It is easier than you might think.

Pick out your song, and possibly your outfit, and follow these quick steps:

Step 1

KNOW what you are performing. (Google the lyrics and compare several versions online). Just because you know the chorus, does not mean you know the meaning of the song. If you understand the meaning, you will better convey the passion of the music.

Step 2

Listen to the song at least ten
times without singing along. It is very important to give your
brain uninterrupted time to HEAR the song. While listening, think about what you would be doing if you were telling someone what is being said in the ltrics. Confused? Almost everyone talks with their hands. Some more than others.

Example of what I would do:

Lyrics - *"The sky was telling me your love."*
Movements - (The sky) My hand would reach for the sky, while my other hand smoothly moved to my mouth (telling me) just before the other moved to my heart (your love).

We call this Choreography. If you take the time to choreograph every single song, for the entire number, you will never be "lost" on stage, you will earn more attention from the audience, and it will surely step up your game, if nothing else.

Step 3

Learn and practice the words and choreography at the same time. Get in the habit of practicing while you ride in the car, sit in your drag room making costumes, stand in bathroom, shower, or in front of a mirror.

If you always associate the words and choreography together, it will provide a more fluid and natural flow on stage. It will take longer to learn your song than normal. It is going to require much more practice, but it can be done!

You do not have to have Natural stage presence to be a great entertainer...

Just FAKE IT!!!

Have a question for Gage or any other writer, email them using the addresses posted on their banners. We can bring you words, but it takes all of you helping us... to bring our words to life. Email us any general questions at

Spotlight@ SpotlightTodayMagazine.com

Continued from Page 30

Mr. Gay North America
International 2012
Sebastian Armonte

What did it mean to win?

Winning and becoming a part of N.A.I. gives me great pride, and affords me the opportunity to give my energy, skills, and experiences to a first class system that believes in giving back...WOW what an honor.

Who is your role model?

Monte St. James, he thinks outside of the box. He takes risks that move the male leads bar to new heights, and made us equal to our counterparts as entertainers.

What got you interested in the North America International Pageant system?

The community involvement "platform" and giving back was the vital reason...N.A.I. is the catalyst for me to enlighten and educate us on bullying, and the long-term impact of the Bullying "platform".

What are your plans for the year of your reign?

During my reign, my objective is to promote all divisions of N.A.I. across the United States, build networks with other systems, grow the contestant's pool, and assist with the logistics for 2013.

What other titles have you held?

I have been blessed and honored to have held the Nationals titles of Mr. Canada International 2006, Mr. Gay All-American 2008, Mr. Gay United States 2009, Mr. USA Unlimited Classique 2009, and Mr. Renaissance 2010.

What advice do you give to those competing in the NAI system?

Advice; do your homework by investigating to determine if your values and goals align with ours, speak with board and court to

Where are you from?

Born in Chicago IL. now residing in Pittsburgh, PA

Miss Gay North America International 2012
Lindsay Paige

gauge insights to how you can take the system to the next level, and how committed and prepared are you to work on behalf of N.A.I.

What is your nonprofit platform and why did you choose it?

Non-profit platform: I was forever changed by the April 20, 1999 tragedy that unfolded at Columbine high school. Combating bullying then and there became my platform. I have spent many hours educating and training school administrators, students, teachers, and parents of the life changing impact that bullying has on the victim, bully, and community as a whole.

How long have you been performing?

Since 1996 and 1999 on the national level.

What did it mean to win?

Winning to me was a dream come true. It gave me the opportunity to be able to travel the country and spread my positive message, and my positive energy to people and communities all over.

Who is your role model?

My role model is my drag mother, Whitney Paige. She took me under her wing as a young entertainer, and has taught me so much about this business, and being a role model myself.

Why the North America International Pageant system?

I originally planned to compete in the Miss International pageant. Then, once I heard about the two systems merging, I decided to research and look into the system. I liked what it stood for, so I entered a prelim.

What are your plans for the year of your reign?

My plans for the year are to travel the country and promote the system to the very best of my ability. I would also like to attend as many national competitions around the country as I possibly can, to show what our system has to offer and work with others who are interested in building our numbers and growth.

What other titles have you held?

Winning this national title was actually my 23rd title. I have won several bar, local, state, and regional titles.

I am a former Miss Gay Oklahoma of America, Miss Gay Oklahoma USofA, Miss Gay Oklahoma USofA at Large, Miss Gay Oklahoma Black America, and Miss Gay Oklahoma Bold and Beautiful; I am the current Miss Diamond Diva of Oklahoma.

Discuss your nonprofit platform?

The platform that I chose for my year is raising money for nonprofit youth organizations around the country. I chose that platform because, as an entertainer, I work with the youth every day in several different places. I feel that it is very important to help groom our youth of today into strong adults of tomorrow.

How long have you been performing?

I have been a female impersonator for the past 11 years. April 12th was my 11th year anniversary as Lindsay Paige.

Where are you from?

I am originally from a small town in South Carolina. I grew up as a military brat, so I spent most of my teenage and adult years in Oklahoma.

Miss Gay North America
International Femme 2012
Asiannah B

What did winning mean to you?

Winning meant the world to me!!! I worked very hard, and was so excited I couldn't think!! I have been through a lot of self-consciousness and put downs in my life, and I had a lot of problems with my weight, but drag helped me to realize that I am beautiful and that my size beautiful, and that I can do anything a skinny girl can do.

Who is your role model?

My role model was, and still is, my mother, Charlotte J Brooks. She was my everything and I strive to be like her one day!!! My drag idol is Anja Mann. In the short amount of time that I have known her, she has taught me so much and has inspired me to keep dancing and performing!!

Why the North America International Pageant system?

My interest in the NAI Pageant system came from the former NAI Femme, Barbie Michaels. She was the first femme that I knew about, and she talked to me all the time about competing. She made me feel like I could do it!! has taught me so much and has inspired me to keep dancing and performing!! Thanks to Barbie!!!

What are your plans for the year of your reign?

My plans are to get a lot of prelims, and get the name Femme out, so that all girls know that no matter what and who you are, you too can compete. Also, I plan to get the name of my platform out to help all the kids that I work with.

What other titles have you held?

I am the current reigning Miss Gay Illinois Femme.

What advice do you give to those competing in the NAI system?

The advice I give to anybody wanting to compete in NAI, is to keep God first, keep calm, and give it your all, and stay truthful to yourself and the system.

Discuss your nonprofit platform?

My platform is Reach One Teach One, which is an inner city foundation through IBPOEofW Elks of the World fraternal group that helps inner city kids by organizing pageants and oratorical contests to win scholarships and cash prizes every year.

How long have you been performing?

I have been performing for 10 months

Now that you know a little about the newly crown National Title holders, find them on facebook. All four new National titleholders are more than willing to answer any questions you may have. The North America International system is organizing State and Regional Prelims in all divisions. The North America International at Large and Supreme Pageant is held this November in Kenosha, Wisconsin.

HAMBURGER
MARY'S
Bar & Grille
EAT, DRINK, AND BE...MARY!
Tampa & Clearwater
Your #1 Destination For
Entertainment 7 Days A Week!
Drag Queen Bingo
Mary's Got Talent
Mary-Oke
Friday & Saturday Night
Diva Revues
Sunday Brunch Shows
Retro Rewind Sundays
Tampa - 1600 E 8th Ave, 813-241-MARY
Clearwater - 28910 US Hwy 19N, 727-400-6996
www.HamburgerMarys.com/Tampa & www.HamburgerMarys.com/Clearwater

Made for a
Queen
We thank the 6,000 plus members of DRAG411
For voting MadeForAQueen.com during their
First Peer Awards "Best Of Drag" the
"Best Online Retailer for Female Impersonators"

520.250.8003
Made for a
Queen
Larry Moore aka Lucinda Holliday

The dozen books
of DRAG411.com
Million Hugs   2011
The Official Drag Handbook
I sent out 2,700 Invites. These Messages Were Sent Back.
Todd Kachinski-Kottmeier   (The Infamous Todd)
DRAG411
Forum
The Official Original Memorial
Best Of DRAG
DRAG PARENTS
Opie
From The People That Created
The Official Drag Handbook
DRAG
Stories
Kings And Queens   Vol. I
Crown
Me!
Todd Kachinski-Kottmeier
DRAG
411
INTERNATIONAL
BENEFITS
GYPSY MOON
Before you build
an empire,
Strengthen your
foundation
Written By Steve Diamond, John Fehr,
Emily Barton, & Todd Kachinski-Kottmeier
Why Me, Harvey Milk?
Todd Kachinski-Kottmeier
DRAG
WORLD
Come Out,
Come Out,
Wherever
You Are
Guerilla
Marketing
Official Drag Handbook

(sic)

Latin adverb: ("thus"; in full: sic erat scriptum, "thus was it written."   Indicates DRAG411 transcribed the comments into this book as found in the original source, complete with any erroneous or archaic spelling or other nonstandard presentation. We try to print the responses using the same words sent to us, ensuring the reader DRAG411 did not change the tone, reflection, or character of each response.

Book of Firsts

**The First Entertainer to become
involved with DRAG411
Naomi Wynters
(Photo By Mark Melnick Photography)**

**The First Entertainer to donate
by purchasing the very first book
Mis Sadistic**

**their own free photo on the
Facebook© DRAG411 Page
Angel gLamar**

**00% of The Advertisements
sold in this magazine was
donated to
The Joshua Tree Feeding Program.
A program feeding HIV families**

Sisters of
Perpetual Indulgence

Posting World's Orders, hoping many of you will become active with this organization in your area. DRAG411 will post what each Order does locally to help change the world, as they send them to us. Though the Sisters do not consider themselves as DRAG in the proper term, we include them to inspire charity. A long time ago, male and female impersonators lead the charge for non-profits. In the past ten years, the drag industry no longer leads. We need heroes, role models, and people to step up in each town. The Sisters primary duty is charity.

Information provided by the Orders.

The Sisters of Perpetual Indulgence (SPI), also called Order of Perpetual Indulgence (OPI) is a charity, protest, and street performance organization that use drag and religious imagery to call attention to sexual intolerance and satirize issues of gender and morality. At their inception in 1979, a small group of gay men in San Francisco began wearing the attire of nuns in visible situations using high camp to draw attention to social conflicts and problems in the Castro District.

The Sisters have grown throughout the U.S. with an international network of orders, which are mostly non-profit charity organizations that raise money for AIDS, LGBT-related causes, and mainstream community service organizations, while promoting safer sex and educating others about the harmful effects of drug use and other risky behaviors.

United States

Mother House
Sisters of Perpetual Indulgence, San Francisco
Founded 1979
584 Castro St., PMB # 392
San Francisco, CA 94114
Tel: 415.820.9697
Contact: TheSisters.Org

ALABAMA

The Magic City Sisters
205 32nd Street South
Birmingham, Al 35233
Fax 205-588-4188
Birmingham, AL 35261
magiccitysistersbham.org

ARIZONA

The Grand Canyon Sisters of Perpetual Indulgence
Founded: 2008
PMB 118 at 5555 North 7th Street, Suite 134
Phoenix, AZ 85014
Email: info@azsisters.org azsisters.org

The Grand Canyon Sisters of Perpetual Indulgence (GCSPI) has the vision to unite, elevate, and empower the Gay, Lesbian, Bisexual and Transgender (GLBT) community throughout Arizona. Our primary role and pledge is cooperative support of every facet of the GLBT community through fundraising, entertainment and education throughout Arizona. The family that created us is the one we honor with our Sacred Sisterly Identity. In 2009, The

Sisters of Perpetual Indulgence celebrated 30 years of comforting the disturbed and disturbing the comfortable. Over the last three decades, The Sisters have grown from a small band of activists and performers in San Francisco to a worldwide organization dedicated to the expiration of stigmatic guilt and the promulgation of universal joy. With houses and missions all over the world, the SPI family is still growing.

CALIFORNIA

Eureka Sisters of Perpetual Indulgence,
Abbey of the Big Red Wood
Founded: 2007
P.O. Box 5625
Eureka, CA 95502-5625
Telephone: (707) 834.4832
Email: sisterfawn@eurekasisters.org
eurekasisters.org

Los Angeles Sisters of Perpetual Indulgence, Inc.
Founded: 1995
8581 Santa Monica Blvd. # 257
West Hollywood, CA 90069
Telephone: (323) 908-3489
lasisters.org

Palm Springs Sisters of Perpetual Indulgence
Palm Springs, California
Founded: 2007
palmspringssisters.org

Russian River Sisters of Perpetual Indulgence, Inc.
Founded: 2000
P.O. Box 771
Guerneville, CA 95446
Telephone: (707) 874-0312
Email: info@rrsisters.org
rrsisters.org

San Diego Sisters of Perpetual Indulgence,
The Asylum of the Tortured Heart
San Diego, California
Founded: 2006
sdsisters.org

FLORIDA

Abbey of St. Gertrude de Nivelles - Orlando
PO Box 3665
Winter Park, Florida 32790-3665
orlandosisters.org

Tampa Bay Sisters of Perpetual Indulgence
Founded: 2008
Post Office Box 11387
St. Petersburg, FL 33733-1387
flsisters.org

GEORGIA

Flaming Sugarbaker Sisters
6141 Queen Anne court
Norcross, GA 30093
atlsisters.org

MASSACHUSETTS

The Boston Sisters,
Convent of the Commonwealth
Boston, Massachusettes
thebostonsisters.org

MISSOURI

The Gateway Sisters of Indulgence
St. Louis, Missouri
gsoistl@gmail.com

NEVADA

Las Vegas Sisters of Perpetual Indulgence,
Holy Order Sin Sity Sisters
Las Vegas, Nevada
Founded: 2006
sinsitysisters.org

Reno's Biggest Little Sisters, Inc.
Reno, Nevada
PO Box 650
Reno, NV 89504
renosbiggestlittlesisters.org

NEW YORK

New York City Sisters
348 Union Street #2
Brooklyn, NY 11231
Email: Agnesknows@aol.com
nycsisters.org

OKLAHOMA

Sisters of the Sacred Heartland
Oklahoma City, OK
okcsisters.org

OREGON

Portland Sisters of Perpetual Indulgence,
The Order of Benevolent Bliss
Portland, Oregon
Founded: 2006
portlandsisters.net

TENNESSEE

Missionary Order of Perpetual Indulgence
Tennessee, Iowa, Chicago, Philadelphia
Founded: 1996
missionarysisters.net

Music City Sisters
Nashville, Tennessee
615-479-8476
MusicCitySisters.org

TEXAS

The DFW Sisters
Dallas/Fort Worth, TX
thedfwsisters.org

WASHINGTON

**The Sisters of Perpetual Indulgence,
The Abbey Of Saint Joan**
Founded: 1996 (1987)
PMB #486
1122 E. Pike St.
Seattle, WA 98122-3934
Telephone: (206) 860-3666
theabbey.org

WISCONSIN

The Abbey of the Brew City Sisters
Milwaukee, Wisconsin
brewcitysisters.org

United States Missions

CALIFORNIA

The River City Sisters
Sacramento, CA

FLORIDA

South Florida Sisters Rising Sun Sisters
Ft. Lauderdale, Florida
myspace.com/southfloridasisters

ILLINOIS

The Abbey of the Windy City Sisters
Chicago, Illinois

OHIO

The Missionary Sisters of Cleveland
Cleveland, Ohio
ohsisters.org

TEXAS

San Antonio Missionary Sisters

INTERNATIONAL
Australia

The Order of Perpetual Indulgence
Sydney, Australia
Founded: 1982
universaljoy.com.au
The Sydney House of the Order of Perpetual Indulgence is the second oldest House in the Universe, and was founded in 1981 by members returning from the Mother House in San Francisco. The Order of Perpetual Indulgence is an International Order and many of the Houses throughout the world have their own modes of dress, manners, traditions, customs, and level of community involvement. Sisters and Brothers, despite their ecclesiastical garb, do get to enjoy themselves and, depending on the occasion, can dress in the most glamorous of habits, all the while taking our mission to expiate stigmatic guilt and promulgate universal joy as a most serious trust. Active throughout the year providing blessings, opening events, and assisting in community activities, the Sydney House nevertheless has a number of more or less fixed activities. These have included the annual Blessing of the Fleet, the blessing of the Dykes on Bikes motorcycles, and participation in the Leather Pride events. Around Mardi Gras these annual events include a presence at Fair Day, an annual History Walk and Zoo Walk as part of the pre Mardi Gras festivities, culminating in our presence in the Parade itself, often accompanied by nuns and brothers from other Australian Houses and from overseas. The Order of Perpetual Indulgence - Sydney House - is always welcoming toward members of the gathered faithful and others who receive the call and would like to join the Order here in Sydney.

The Order of Perpetual Indulgence in Australia, Inc
Adelaide, Australia
Founded: 1992

Canada

Abbey of the Long Cedar Canoe Society
Vancouver, BC
Founded 2010
yvrsisters.ca

Colombia

Hermanitas de la Perpetua Indulgencia
Seccional, Colombia
hermanitas.8m.com

France

Les Soeurs de la Perpétuelle Indulgence,
Couvent de Paris
Paris, France
Founded: 1989
lessoeurs.org

Les Soeurs de Perpétuelle Indulgence,
Couvent de Paname
Paris, France
Founded: 1996
couventdepaname.org

Les Soeurs de Perpétuelle Indulgence,
Couvent des Chenaies
Marseille, Aix-en-Provence, Lyon,
Nice; France
SPI / Couvent des Chenaies
c/o Didier Pugliese
2695 avenue du Colonel Maurice Bellec
13540 Puyricard
France
20six.fr/spi-chenaies

Germany

Orden der Schwestern der Perpetuellen Indulgenz e.V.,
Erzmutterhaus Sankta Melitta Iuvenis zu Berlin
Fonded: 1991 (1993, 2003; Reunion of S.P.I. and O.P.I. Berlin in 2007)
O.S.P.I. e.V. Berlin
Blücherstr. 26 B
D-10961 Berlin
Germany
erzmutterhaus@indulgenz.de
indulgenz.de

Die Schwestern der Perpetuellen Indulgenz zu Hamburg
Haus Notre Dame Sainte Diana
Founded: 1996
S.P.I. Hamburg
c/o Hein & Fiete
Pulverteich 21
D-20099
Hamburg, Germany
info@spihamburg.de
spihamburg.de

Die Schwestern der Perpetuellen Indulgenz e.V.
Haus Sancta Maria Penetrantia
Founded: 1997
S.P.I. e.V. Köln
Adam - Stegerwald - Strasse 32
51063 Köln

Germany
Telephone: +49 221 - 88 74 314
info@spicologne.de
www.spicologne.de

Die Schwestern der Perpetuellen Indulgenz
Erzabtei zum Westfälischen Frieden e.V.
Abbey Peace of Westphalia eV
c/o P. Abe Supreme Vöhde 114
44575 Castrop-Rauxel
www.spi-westfalen.de

Spendensammlungen
Bei unserer Arbeit sammeln wir immer Spenden. Das Geld kommt zu drei Vierteln
Hilfsprojekten zugute, um damit Menschen mit HIV und AIDS zu unterstützen. Mit dem
letzten Viertel finanzieren wir unsere Arbeitsmaterialien wie Kondome, Gleitgel, Red Ribbon,
Flyer etc.
Seit dem Jahr 2007 haben wir den Kreis unsere Spendennehmer erweitert, da wir HIV / Aids
und Prävention nicht als solitäre Probleme sehen. Eine gesamt-gesundheitliche Sichtweise
und eine allgemeine Aufklärung über Sexualität, sowie der Möglichkeiten diese Auszuleben,
ist Voraussetzung für ein verantwortliches und selbstbewustes Handeln bei Safer Sex.
Gerade im Umgang mit einer bestehenden Infektion oder vermuteten Erkrankungen, ist eine
stabile Lebensgrundlage und die Möglichkeit zum Informationsaustausch eine wichtige
Grundlage.
Aus diesem Grunde unterstützen wir auch Selbsthilfe- und Aufklärungsprojekte, die dazu
beitragen dieses Fundament für die Präventionsarbeit zu legen.

Spenden
Wir würden uns sehr freuen, wenn Du unsere Arbeit mit einer Spende direkt unterstützt.
Gerne stellen wir auf Wunsch hierfür auch eine Spendenbescheinigung aus.
Spendenkonto:
Die Schwestern der Perpetuellen Indulgenz
Kontonummer: 180 009
Bankleitzahl: 370 605 90
SPARDA Bank Köln e.G.

Scotland

The Order of Perpetual Indulgence,
Convent of Dunn Eideann
Edinburgh, Scotland
P.O. Box 666
Edinburgh
EH7 5YW
www.thesisters.org.uk/

The Order of Perpetual Indulgence,
Convent of Moravia
2-4 Lamb Street, Elgin IV30 2DG
www.thesisters.org.uk/

Switzerland

Der Orden der Perpetuellen Indulgenz
Zürich, Switzerland www.derorden.ch
Der Orden
Archetypus Nonne
Nonnen haben in allen Jahrhunderten ihre Arbeitsleistung ihren Mitmenschen zur Verfügung
gestellt. Sie tun dies selbstlos und aus innerer Überzeugung in verschiedenen Bereichen wie
Forschung, Bildung sowie Alten- und Krankenpflege.
Habit
Unser schillerndes Ornat ist die Brücke, die die Menschen an unsere Arbeit heranführt. Es
erregt die Aufmerksamkeit für unsere Ordensziele. Das weiß grundierte Gesicht symbolisiert
den Tod, die bunten Farben das Leben und die Lebensfreude.
Die Leistung unseres Ordens
Wir sammeln Spenden für Hilfsprojekte zu HIV und AIDS, betreiben Primärprävention und
halten das Thema "AIDS" in der Öffentlichkeit wach. Wir sind wie exotische Schmetterlinge,
die lebensbejahend zu den Menschen flattern und versuchen, ihnen Freude zu bereiten.

United Kingdom

The House of Common Sluts
London, United Kingdom   www.londonsisters.org

The Sisters of Perpetual Indulgence,
Manchester, United Kingdom www.thesisters.demon.co.uk

The Sisters of Perpetual Indulgence, Sussex
Sussex, United Kingdom

The Abbey of the Dreaming Spires
Oxford, United Kingdom

The Sanctuary of the Sisters of Perepetual Contumaciousness
Rockall, United Kingdom

Uruguay
Uruguay Convento Mater Admirabilis
Orden de San Felipe y Santiago de Montevideo
Parroquia de la Inmaculada de Jádraque
San Felipe y Santiago de Montevideo, Uruguay
www.perpetuaindulgencia.tk

**100% of The Advertisements sold in this magazine were
donated to The Joshua Tree Feeding Program.
A program feeding HIV familie**

Thousands of votes from around the world marked the largest peer award in LGBT history for the Drag Industry reaching for the title of "Best of Drag" as determined by the members of their own craft. Many people voted for themselves, some people did not vote for a single person as being worthy of accreditation, a couple tried to cheat, but in the long run the first annual award was certified.

DRAG411 hopes this October more people will honor the teams of people around them, helping them become a success. We thank the wonderful community leaders for stepping in to count the ballots and certify the votes before handing the results over to Todd Kachinski Kottmeier (Drag411 Founder) and the BecHavn Publishing team.

If you do not agree with the results, grab ten of your friends in the industry and simply ask, "Who received your vote?" We sent out over 6,000 invitations, begged attention in over 62 Facebook© groups and pages we managed in 2013, plus an additional 112 we use as mentors, and posted with every ballot, an invitation to invite your own peer friends.

International   Peer   Award   Ballot Requirements to vote:

This was the International Peer Award ballot provided to every single drag related business, group, and organization in 32 countries. DRAG411 also provided it not only to over 6,000 male and female impersonators retired or active around the world, but asked with every step "for those reading the posts and messages" to invite peers around them, to honor THE BEST OF DRAG. If you did not receive a ballot, it was not because DRAG411 failed to reach out. We are also active on over one hundred Facebook© groups and pages (and admin or founded sixty-two of them). The deadline each year is Thanksgiving Day. Ballots are posted on October 18th each year. Over 5,000 votes cast in the First Annual International DRAG411 "Best of Drag" Peer Award. Auditors verified the identity and position of every single voter.

NOTE: *Private letters received by stunned "non-winners" questioning, "Why they did not win?" Each was saddened to realize their own peers did not cast votes for them; after all, it is a peer award, much like a People's Choice amongst the industry. I asked, "Did you even vote for yourself in this category?" I doubt George Bush went into the poll and voted for Obama. "If you do not have faith in voting for yourself, how can you expect others to follow? Perhaps next time… perhaps.*

Name of your favorite local show bar for male impersonators
Winner: **Hamburger Mary's**

Wildest KING
Vicious Slick

Most charitable KING (for charity)
Vinnie Marconi

2013 Winners. Who will win in 2014?

Favorite KING Fundraiser involving the drag community
Kings for a Cause

Best Dressed KING
Tied Vote
Baron von Ausome   **Freddy Prinze Charming**

KING with the most creative wardrobe
Tied Vote
Justin Case   **Landon Cider**

KING with the wildest hair
Vincent Von Dyke

KING with the best stage productions
Anson Reign

Best Bar or Venue for a King Pageant
Tied
Angles   **Rainbow Cactus**

Best KING Pageant system representing your local community
Mister Phoenix Pride

Best KING Pageant system representing your State or Region
Mister USofA Arizona

Best National KING Pageant system
Mister USofA MI (Male Illusionist)

Best Judge for a KING Pageant
Gunner Gatlyn
Best entertainer to host a KING pageant
Nobody earned two votes.

Favorite National KING Pageant Winner
Ivory Onyx

Best Region with the best KINGS
Tampa Bay

Most Inspiring KING
Anson Reign

Funniest KING
Vinnie Marconi

The Biggest Role Model as a KING
(Can only win Role Model once.
For lifetime accomplishments)
Anson Reign

King of the Year: 2013
(Can only win King of the Year once.
For Accomplishments only in 2013)
Landon Cider

2013 Homecoming King,
Best representing your Local Drag Community
(Can only win Homecoming King once.
For lifetime accomplishments)
Freddy Prinze Charming

Name of your favorite local show bar for female impersonators
BS West

Best all-around QUEEN
Amy DeMilo

Wildest QUEEN
Pandora DeStrange

Most Charitable QUEEN (for charity)
Tied
Afeelya Bunz   Barbara Seville

Favorite QUEEN Fundraiser involving the drag community
Barbra Seville's Wonderful 100 AIDS Walk

Most Creative QUEEN
Celia Putty

Best lip synch by a QUEEN
Coco Montrese

Best Dressed QUEEN
Chad Michaels
QUEEN with the most creative wardrobe
Celia Putty

QUEEN with the wildest wardrobe
Sizzel Lamour

QUEEN with the wildest hair
Felicia Minor

QUEEN with the best stage productions
ShaeShae LaReese

Best Bar or Venue for a QUEEN Pageant
BS West

Best QUEEN Pageant system representing your local community
Tied
Miss Phoenix Pride   **Miss BS West**

Best lip synch by a KING
Vinnie Marconi

Best QUEEN Pageant system representing your State or Region
No single state system won five votes for their state

Best National QUEEN Pageant system
USofA

Best all-around KING
Landon Cider

Best Judge for a QUEEN Pageant
Mike Fornelli

Best entertainer to host a QUEEN pageant
Bob Taylor

Favorite National QUEEN Pageant Winner
Catia Lee Love

Region with the best QUEENS
Tampa Bay

Most Inspiring QUEEN
Nova Starr

Funniest QUEEN
Lucinda Holiday

The Biggest Role Model as a QUEEN
RuPail

QUEEN of the Year: 2013
(Can only win QUEEN of the Year once.
For Accomplishments only in 2013)
Tied
Erica Andrews   **Pandora DeStrange**

QUEEN of QUEENS
Lifetime Achievement Award
(Can only win QUEEN of QUEENS once.
For lifetime accomplishments)
RuPaul

2013 Homecoming QUEEN
Best representing your Local Drag Community
(Can only win Homecoming QUEEN once.
For lifetime accomplishments)
Barbra Seville

Best place to buy padding
Boom Boom LaRue's

Best QUEEN Troupe creating productions in 2013
Arizona Gender Outlaws

Best KING Troupe creating productions in 2013
Sisterz Twisted

Best QUEEN Drag Website not on Facebook©
ArizonaDrag.com

KING with the wildest wardrobe
Baron von Ausome

Best KING NON-FACEBOOK© Drag Website in 2013
KingsforaCause.weebly.com

Favorite past RuPaul Contestant (since the beginning)
Latrice Royale

<Latrice also won Most DRAG411 Shares on Facebook© for Female Impersonators while Rasta Boi Punany won for male impersonator with the most shares. The Grand Canyon Sisters of Perpetual Indulgence won for group with most shares, taking the lead with a total so high, it beat the other top one hundred individuals combined.>

Best Drag KING Shopping Group on Facebook©
Boy Drag Depot

Best Drag QUEEN Shopping Group on Facebook©
6SBoutique

Best Support Group for KINGS
Drag King Network on Facebook©

Best Support Group for Queens
Drag Queen Beginners on Facebook©

Best Show Venue for a new KING to get a break in 2013
No venue received three votes

King of Kings / Lifetime Achievement Award
(Can only win King of Kings once.
For lifetime accomplishments)
Anson Reign

Best Show Venue for a new QUEEN to get a break in 2013
BS West

Best KING Show Venue Audience in 2013
Hamburger Mary's TAMPA

Best QUEEN Show Venue Audience in 2013
Hamburger Mary's TAMPA

Favorite Organization using MALE IMPERSONATION
As a theme, to raise money for charity in 2013
Kings for a Cause

Favorite Organization using FEMALE IMPERSONATION
As a theme, to raise money for charity in 2013
Grand Canyon Sisters of Perpetual Indulgence

Best place to buy over-all make up
Boom Boom LaRue's   **6SBoutique**

Best place or person to buy completed jewelry
Nova Starr

Best place to buy breasts
Boom Boom LaRue's

Best place to download music
YouTube

Favorite person creating re-mix music
Boy George

Number one place YOU SHOP to buy KING drag clothes.
Goodwill

Number one place YOU SHOP to buy QUEEN drag clothes
Goodwill

Best "in-store" retailer spoiling KINGS
6SBoutique

Best "in-store" retailer spoiling QUEENS
6SBoutique

Best "online" " retailer spoiling KINGS
6SBoutique

Best "online" retailer spoiling QUEENS
Made for a Queen

Best Seamster/Seamstress for a KING
India Ferrah

Best Seamster/Seamstress for a QUEEN
India Ferrah

Best place for colored contacts
6SBoutique

Best Makeup Artist for QUEENS (No winner for Kings)
Pandora DeStrange

Favorite place to buy drag shoes
Goodwill

Best photographer for KINGS
Alex Melo

Best photographer for QUEENS
Kristopher Reynolds

Most famous local KING
Freddy Prinze Charming

Most famous local QUEEN
Pandora Boxx

Best of 2013 King Event.
Kings for a Cause
Best of 2013 Queen Event
Not one event by female impersonators received three votes

Most involved and dedicated Spouse of KING
Ali Daugherty-Sturmer

Most involved and dedicated Spouse of QUEEN
Josh Kline

Best Licensed Promoter of QUEENS *(No winner for Kings.)*
All Starr Management

Best place to "just hang out as a KING"
Rainbow Cactus

Best place to "just hang out as a QUEEN"
Hamburger Mary's TAMPA

Best DJ for a show
Josh Kline

Best Internet Drag Show hosted by a KING or QUEEN (or both)
Let's Have a Fefe

Record Shares On Facebook

The Grand Canyon Sisters of Perpetual Indulgence (GCSPI) hold the DRAG411 Share record on Facebook© for the following photo"

"Westboro showed up in force for Phoenix Pride. To protect them the police department placed them behind a restricted barricade. Notice the Grand Canyon Sisters of Perpetual Indulgence holding up massive banners to block them behind the flags. I believe all of us should repeat this in all our states! Please share to get the word out."

International Imperial Court System
(IICS)

Posting World's Courts, hoping many of you will become active with this organization in your area. DRAG411 will post what each Court does locally to help change the world, as they send them to us. Though the Courts do not consider themselves as DRAG in the proper term, we include them to inspire charity. A long time ago, male and female impersonators lead the charge for non-profits. In the past ten years, the drag industry no longer leads. We need heroes, role models, and people to step up in each town. The primary duty of the Court System is charity.

Information provided by the Courts

The International Imperial Court System (IICS) is one of the oldest and largest gay organizations in the world. The court raises money for charity through large annual fancy-dress costume balls in communities throughout North America and numerous smaller fundraisers each year. Members of the group have said it is the second largest gay organization in the world, surpassed only by the Metropolitan Community Church.

Canada

Regal Social Association of Regina
2345 St. John Street
Regina, Saskatchewan S4P 1S7
Canada
courtreginacanada@yahoo.com

United States

California
IMPERIAL COURT DE SAN DIEGO
The Imperial Court of San Diego is a 501c3 not-for-profit organization that has donated millions of dollars since its inception in 1973. The primary mission of the Imperial Court of San Diego is to raise funds for LGBT- and HIV/AIDS related charities and the Community at large. The Court, a 501(c)3 corporation, has raised over two million dollars in its forty-one years for such worthy causes as Mama's Kitchen, LGBT Family Matters, The Center S.D. Toni Akins Lesbian Health Fund, Scott Carlson Thanksgiving Dinner, Tijuana Aids Fund, The Benjamin F. Dillingham III Community Grant. Annual Blanket Drive, The Queen Eddie Youth, The Harvey Milk / Nicole Murray Ramirez Student Scholarship Program The Annual LGBT Community, Easter Egg Hunt, Kid's Toy Drive, , Christy's Place, and Being Alive, among many others. We also visit the AIDS ward at UCSD Hospital for the Holidays.

Kentucky
IMPERIAL COURT OF KENTUCKY
P.O. Box 265
Lexington, KY 40588
The Imperial Court of Kentucky, Inc. is a 501(c)3 nonprofit charity with a special outreach to the GLBT community of Kentucky. Founded in 1982 and based on the savants of manner of English royalty, the Imperial Court of Kentucky is a charter member of the International Court System with over 70 other courts across North America. The Court provides a social outlet and recognition to the GLBT community and its supporters through frequent events, such as the Falsie Awards, all while raising funds for local charitable causes. In 2006, The Imperial Court of Kentucky was named International Court of Distinction by the International Court Council.
info@imperialcourtkentucky.org

New York
IMPERIAL COURT OF NEW YORK

The Imperial Court of New York is a 501c3 not-for-profit organization that has donated millions of dollars since its inception in 1986. The primary mission of the Imperial Court of New York is to raise funds for LGBT- and HIV/AIDS related charities. The Court, a 501(c)3 corporation, has raised over two million dollars in its twenty-four years for such worthy causes as amfAR's HIV/AIDS Treatment Directory, Bailey House, God's Love We Deliver, Broadway Cares/Equity Fights AIDS, Harvey Milk School, the LGBT Community Services Center, LIFEbeat (The Music Industry Fights AIDS), PFLAG (Parents, Families & Friends of Lesbians & Gays), SAGE (Services & Advocacy for GLBT Elders), and Sylvia's Place (a refuge for homeless gay youth), among many others. We also bring live entertainment to AIDS hospices in the metropolitan area.

We do this in our own unique fashion, by producing entertaining fund-raising events throughout the year. Some are small shows and others are major productions, including our most famous event, Night of a Thousand Gowns, a charity ball and silent auction held each spring. Attracting about 1,000 guests, the ball is a gala social event of the gay charity calendar. In addition, we lend our support to other organizations for their own fund-raising efforts. Our membership includes Lords and Ladies, Dukes and Duchesses, Princes and Princesses, and an Emperor and Empress, all enjoying the "game" of court and royalty while raising much needed social awareness and monies for deserving charities on local, national and international levels. We cannot do it alone. We need the support of the community and especially the support of the generous organizations that share our dedication to these worthy causes as well as a love for the humor and high camp we uniquely bring to our every endeavor. Help us put the "fun" in fundraising.

Imperial Court Of All Alaska
PO Box 202353
Anchorage, AK 99520-2353

Imperial Court of Arizona
PO Box 36834
Phoenix, AZ 85067-6834

Imperial Sovereign Court of The Czarist Dynasty
PO Box 9106
Chico, CA 95927

Imperial Star Empire, Inc.
Alameda/Contra Costa Counties California
P.O. Box 55486
Hayward, CA 94545

Royal Grand Ducal Council
Of Alameda/Contra Costa Counties, Inc.
PO Box 4561
Hayward, CA 94540-4561

Imperial Court of Los Angeles/Hollywood
PO Box 2301
Hollywood, CA 90078

International Imperial Court of Long Beach
PO Box 20355

Long Beach, CA 90801

Owl Empire of Stanislaus County
PO Box 580030
Modesto, CA 95350

Court of the Great Northwest Empire
2000 K Street
Sacramento, CA 95811-4217

Imperial Court de San Diego
PO Box 34104
San Diego, CA 92163

Council Grand Duke and Duchesses of San Francisco
PO Box 420905
San Francisco, CA 94142-0905

Imperial Council of San Francisco
584 Castro Street
San Francisco, CA 94114-2512

Imperial Royal Lion Monarchy
PO Box 53253
San Jose, CA 95153

Imperial San Joaquin Delta Empire
PO Box 690333
Stockton, CA 95204-4911

Orange County Imperial Court
PO Box 11332
Westminster, CA 92685-1332

United Court of the Pike Peak's Empire
PO Box 6925
Colorado Springs, CO 80904

Imperial Court of the Rocky Mountain Empire
PO Box 2108
Denver, CO 80202

Imperial Sovereign of All Connecticut
PO Box 4427
Hartford, CT 06147-4427

Imperial Court of Washington, DC
PO Box 2616
Washington, DC 20013

Imperial Court of Hawaii
1320 Middle St
Honolulu, HI 96819

Imperial Court Of Iowa
PO Box 1491
Des Moines, IA 50306-1491

Imperial Sovereign Gem Court Of Idaho
PO Box 6338
Boise, ID 83707-6338

Imperial Windy City Court of the Prairie State Empire
PO Box 804545
Chicago, IL 60680-4107
Imperial Court of Kentucky
PO Box 265
Lexington, KY 40588

Imperial Court Of Massachusetts
Royal Commonwealth Society
PO Box 51095
Boston, MA 02205

Imperial Sovereign Court of Minnesota
PO Box 582601
Minneapolis, MN 55458

Court of the Many Rivers of King Louis XIV
PO Box 19018
St. Louis, MO 63118

Imperial Sovereign Court of Montana
PO Box 4681
Missoula, MT 59806-4681

Imperial Court of Nebraska
PO Box 3772
Omaha, NE 68103

United Court Of The Sandias, Inc.
PO Box 80343
Albuquerque, NM 87198-0343

Imperial Court of the Desert Empire
PO Box 46481
Las Vegas, NV 89114

Silver Dollar Court, Inc.
PO Box 6581
Reno, NV 89513

Imperial Court Of Buffalo
266 Elmwood Ave #187
Buffalo, NY 14222

Imperial Court of New York
PO Box 613

New York, NY 10116-0613

Imperial Sovereign Queen City Court of The Buckeye Empire
PO Box 141152
Cincinnati, OH 45250

Imperial Court of All Oklahoma, Inc.
PO Box 14533
Tulsa, OK 74159

We are the Oklahoma Chapter of the International Imperial Court System. We are a Nonprofit 501(c)(3) charitable fundraising organization operating in the State of Oklahoma, FOR the People of Oklahoma. Our goal is to unite the People of Oklahoma, and the organizations serving the People through love, understanding, education, service, and fraternity

Imperial Sovereign Court of the Emerald Empire
PO Box 3243
Eugene, OR 97403

Imperial Sovereign Rose Court
PO Box 4864
Portland, OR 97208

Imperial Sovereign Court of the Willamette Empire
PO Box 2263
Salem, OR 97308-2263

Imperial Court of Rhode Island
PO Box 6583
Providence, RI 02940

United Court of Austin
PO Box 2567
Austin, TX 78768-2567

Royal Sovereign Imperial Court of The Texas Riviera Empire
PO Box 3882
Corpus Christi, TX 78463-3882

United Court of the Lone Star Empire
PO Box 190865
Dallas, TX 75219-0865

Imperial Court of de Fort Worth/Arlington
PO Box 365
Fort Worth, TX 76101

Empire of the Royal Sovereign Imperial Court of the Single Star
PO Box 980444
Houston, TX 77098-0444

Royal, Sovereign & Imperial Court of the Alamo Empire
PO Box 120111

San Antonio, TX 78212-9311

Royal, Sovereign and Imperial Court of The Central Texas Empire, Inc.
PO Box 20761
Waco, TX 76702-0761

Imperial Rainbow Court of Northern Utah
PO Box 3131
Ogden, UT 84409-3131

Royal Court of the Golden Spike Empire
PO Box 11793
Salt Lake City, UT 84147-0793

Imperial Sovereign Court of The Evergreen Empire
PO Box 5809
Bellingham, WA 98227-5809

Imperial Court of Everett
PO Box 5612
Lynwood, WA 98406

Imperial Sovereign Court of Seattle and the Olympic and Rainier Empire
1122 E. Pike #1300
Seattle, WA 98122

Imperial Sovereign Court of Spokane
PO Box 65
Spokane, WA 99210-0065

Imperial Sovereign Court of Tacoma Diamond Empire of the Cascades
PO Box 488
Tacoma,   WA 98401

Imperial Sovereign Court of the Raintree Empire
PO Box 966
Vancouver, WA 98666

Imperial Sovereign Court of the Chinook Arch
PO Box 23155
Calgary, AB T2P 3B1
CANADA

Imperial Sovereign Court of the Wild Rose
PO Box 11394
Edmonton, AB T5J 3K6
CANADA

Imperial Sovereign Court of Surrey - Empire of the Peace Arch
PO Box 33557
Surrey, BC V3T 5R5
CANADA

Dogwood Monarchist Society
PO Box 204
Vancouver, BC V6E 4L2
CANADA

Imperial Sovereign Court of Winnipeg and All of Manitoba
PO Box 26053
Winnipeg, MB R3G 0M4
CANADA

Imperial & Sovereign Court of Atlantic Nova Society, Inc.
PO Box 36098
Halifax, NS B3J 3S9
CANADA

Imperial Court of Hamilton-Wentworth
PO Box 57177
Hamilton, ON L8P 4X2
CANADA

Royal Imperial Sovereign Court of London Southwestern Ontario Inc
PO Box 44021
London,   ON N6A 5S5
CANADA

Imperial Sovereign Court of St. Catharine's and the Greater Niagara Region
PO Box 23073
St. Catherine's, ON L2R 7P6
CANADA

The Imperial Court of Toronto
PO Box 46
Toronto, ON M4Y 2H0
CANADA

Regal Social Association of Regina
2345 St. John Street
Regina, SK S4P 1S7
CANADA

100% of The Advertisements sold in this magazine were donated to The Joshua Tree Feeding Program.

Thank You!

I thank Miguel Valverde and Michael Oehler for volunteering to run
the DRAG411.com and Hot Shot! Jello Shot Program to benefit
The Joshua Tree Program. On behalf of all the Joshua Tree families,
I also thank the thousands of male and female impersonators around
the world for donating their time and words to help us feed
HIV/AIDS families without once ever demanding payment or gifts.
Todd Kachinski Kottmeier, founder DRAG411 and Hot Shots!

AUTHOR & ENTREPRENEUR
JENETTHA J. BAINES
100 of the MOST INFLUENTIAL Gay Entertainers VOLUME 2
100 of the MOST INFLUENTIAL Gay Entertainers
JENETTHA J. BAINES
100 of the MOST INFLUENTIAL
Gay Entertainers
VOL. 1&2
ORDER YOUR COPY TODAY!
WWW.100MIGE.COM

RuPaul's Girls!

The Basic Low Down of RuPaul's Girls
By Joseph A Gaxiola

SHOW ONE OF THREE: RuPaul's Drag Race

Season One

Episode One

Nine drag queens from around the nation were picked for the first ever RuPauls' Drag Race. Those nine queens are; Akashia, BeBe Zahara Benet, Jade, Nina Flowers, Ongina, Rebecca Glasscock, Shannel, and Victoria "Porkshop" Parker. The queens arrive in full drag to meet each other. No sooner that they meet each other they have their first mini-challenge. A car wash/ photo shoot with Mike Ruiz. The queens' first elimination challenge involves making an outfit out of thrift store clothes and accessories from a 99-cent store. We are introduced to the three permanent judges of RuPaul's Drag Race, Santino Rice, Merle Ginsberg and RuPaul. At every judging there will be two guest judges to fill out the judging panel. At the judging the queen will be judged on their outfits and the photos, they took with Mike Ruiz. Nina Flowers won the first judging. For the final test the bottom two queens will "lip-sync for their lives" to stay in the competition. Akashia and Victoria were in the bottom two in which Victoria lost and RuPaul sent home.

Episode Two

The eight remaining queens next mini-challenge is to take selfies with a digital camera while acting out certain emotions. Akashia and Ongina was the mini-challenge and become the leaders of the next main challenge – girl groups. The first "girl group" consisted of Ongina, Shannel, Nina, and Rebecca. The second "girl group" consisted of Akashia, Bebe, Jade and Tammie. Each group would be responsible for hair, makeup, costumes and choreography. The songs that were picked are from Destiny's Child. At judging the guest judges were Frank Gatson and Michelle Williams. Each group performed their number and Ongina's "girl group" won the main challenge and Ongina was the overall winner. The bottom two queens were Akashia and Tammie. During lip-syncing, Tammie decided to give up and not lip-sync at all. So Tammie RuPaul sent home.

Episode Three

The seven remaining queens are told their main challenge was to evoke Oprah Winfrey. The challenge is in three parts. The first part is become a newscaster where the queens had to read news stories from the teleprompter. The second part is sell products for their "*My Favorite Things*" A RuPaul version momicking a segment done on Oprah Winfrey's show. The third part is to interview Tori Spelling and Dean McDermott. At judging the guest judges are Howard Bragman and Debra Wilson. The judges got to see the video of the Oprah challenge and declared that BeBe was the winner. The bottom two queens were Shannel and Akashia. Akashia RuPaul sent home.

Episode Four

When the six remaining queens came into the workroom all of the mirrors were covered. The mini-challenge was the queens each other's makeup. Jade won the mini-challenge. The main challenge was the girls making a commercial for Mac's Viva Glam makeup. During the commercial, the girls explained why they are, why they are beautiful, and how Viva Glam is helping people who are living with the HIV virus. At judging the guest judges are Gordon Espinet and Jenny Shimizu. The judges saw each queen's commercial and declaring Ongina the winner. Ongina started to cry and stated that she has been living with HIV for the past two years. The bottom two queens were Rebecca and Jade to which Jade was eliminated.

Episode Five

The remaining five queens' next mini-challenge is to bring in five female fighters to put the queens through as exercise challenge. Rebecca was the queen who won this challenge. The main challenge is the queens to make over the five female fighters and teach them the art of drag. Since Rebecca won the mini-challenge she got to choose which queens would be paired with the female fighters. In addition, the queens must also coach the female fighters on how to lip-sync Beyonce's "Freakum Dress" on stage. At judging the guest judges are Lucy Lawless and Robin Antin. After the comparing the female fighters makeovers and watching their lip-syncing, Rebecca was named the winner of the main challenge. The bottom two queens were BeBe and Ongina. After lip-syncing RuPaul left the set to think things through because both queens were too good to pick a winner. Ultimately, it was Ongina who was eliminated.

Episode Six

The remaining four queens met RuPaul on the runway stage for a vogue mini-challenge. RuPaul declares Nina the winner of the mini-challenge. The main challenge for the queens is to have a drag ball. Each queen must come up with three different looks for the stage; swimsuit, executive realness, and evening wear. The queens were also informed that Absolut was sponsoring the drag ball and each queen was given a flavor by Nina. At judging, the quest-judges were Jeffrey Moran and Maria Conchita Alonso. After showing off their three looks RuPaul asked each queen, who should be the next queen to leave the show. Rebecca states Shannel should go both Nina and BeBe say that Rebecca should go but Shannel says she should go because the judges have been too critical on her compared to everyone else. BeBe won the main challenge and Shannel was eliminated.

Episode Seven

This is a "looking back" episode. Showing footage that has been aired as well as footage that did not make it to the series, they also show the audition videos of the queens who made it on the show. They also showed videos of the queens who did not make it on the show. Permanent judges Santino Rice and Merle Ginsberg stated their Top 10 picks of the fashions of this past season.

Episode Eight

The remaining three queens were informed by Merle and Santino that their last challenge is to appear in RuPaul's video "Cover Girl (Put The Bass In Your Walk)." In the video, the three queens will perform in a group dance, record a verse by rapping and film a solo dance. BeBe, Nina and Rebecca learn the choreography from Ryan Heffington. Then each queen sits down with RuPaul and discusses their inner thoughts and feelings. At the final judging there were no guest judges only Santino, Merle and RuPaul. The judges looked at the video clips featuring the last three queens. The three judges compared the final three queens with each other as well as how they were in all of the different challenges this past season. Rebecca was eliminated and came in third place. The final two, BeBe and Nina, had to lip-sync a number to win RuPaul's Drag Race. After the number RuPaul announces that BeBe Zahara Benet is the first ever RuPaul's Drag Race Winner!

Episode Nine

The Reunion Show; the nine queens gather once again to talk about this past season. The first four queens to be on stage were Victoria, Tammie, Akashia, and Jade. RuPaul asks Victoria if she enjoyed her short stay and if she felt she could have done well in the later challenges. Tammie discusses her quirkiness. Akashia's anger and tearful exit are touched on. Jade voices her frustration with Rebecca and her joy in meeting the other girls.Then the next three queens brought up on stage are Ongina, Shannel, and Rebecca. Ongina talks about her outing as an HIV positive person in Episode Four. Shannel's elimination against Rebecca was discussed. Finally, the last two queens were brought up on stage; Nina Flowers and BeBe Zahara Benet. Nina talks about finishing second. BeBe talks about winning. RuPaul asks BeBe if she was surprised that Rebecca made it to the final three and when asked for hands, most queens feel she shouldn't have. Merle Ginsberg and Santino Rice are brought out to discuss their experiences on the show. Merle talks about everyone's ideas of femininity and Santino discusses the fashion and his judging style. The girls are then allowed to get into the judges' heads and Shannel says she left the show because Santino made her feel like crap every week. Ongina says negative critiques can sometimes override positive ones and Akashia says she had never had problems with Santino. Nina Flowers is crowned Miss Congeniality.

<u>**Season Two**</u>

Episode One

This season 12 drag queens from around the nation were picked for the second season of RuPauls' Drag Race. The 12 queens are; Jessica Wild, Jujubee, Morgan McMichaels, Mystique Summers Madison, Nicole Paige Brooks, Pandora Boxx, Raven, Sahara Davenport, Shangela Laquifa Wadley, Sonique, Tatianna, and Tyra Sanchez.We discovered that some of the queens knew each other prior to the show. RuPaul shows up to greet the new queens and tell them about their first mini-challenge – a photo-shoot with Mike Ruiz in a "Gone with the Wind" theme. The first main challenge consists of 12 window treatments with different style curtains. Each queen has to choose one and make an outfit made entirely of the curtains. Raven is allowed to select her curtains first as a reward for having the best photo, but the other queens must race one another to grab one of the available window treatments. On the judging panel RuPaul, Merle Ginsberg, and Santino Rice return as regular judges. Mike Ruiz and Kathy Griffin are the guest judges. The winner of the challenge was Morgan McMichaels. The bottom two were Sahara Davenport and Shangela Laquifa Wadley.

Episode Two

The queens were given a mini-challenge where they are split into teams of two and asked to give a RuPaul doll a "bad girl" makeover. RuPaul selects Sahara and Pandora as the winners, and they are made group leaders for the next challenge. For the main challenge, the contestants will be split into two teams and create a burlesque performance for a Hollywood nightclub. RuPaul reveals a twist not only will the teams take turns performing on stage at the Hollywood club Dragonfly, but they'll also take turns selling cherry pie gift certificates from Café Audrey to people on the street. The team that makes the most money in tips at the club and in gift certificates outside will be the winner. Judging their performances in the club are the show's regular judges along with Kim Coles and Dita Von Teese as the guest judges. At the judging panel Sahara Davenport's team, RuPaul declared as having earned the most money during the challenge. Sahara is also announced as being the challenge winner for leading her team. Raven and Nicole Paige Brooks are in the bottom two and have to "lip-synch for their lives". Raven is saved from elimination and Nicole Paige Brooks is sent home.

Episode Three

The queens' next mini-challenge is a blind taste test of three foods. They have to guess if what they ate was chicken or some other fried food. The three queens with the most points are Pandora, Mystique and Morgan. As a tiebreaker, the three contestants raced to see who could eat a basket of fried chicken, rabbit, alligator and deep fried cow brains the fastest. Mystique and Morgan are declared the winners. They become captains and have to form their teams for the main challenge. The main challenge tasked the two groups with creating a commercial for Disco Extra Greasy Shortening. Mystique's team creating a commercial for fish fillets, and Morgan's team creating a commercial for fried chicken. RuPaul reveals a twist: the queens need to swap scripts, forcing them to change their entire performance immediately. During the commercial taping, Kathy Najimy serves as co-director and coaches the girls through the commercial. At the judging panel, the guest judges are Kathy Najimy and Tanya Tucker. After watching the commercials, RuPaul tells them that they will be critiqued individually rather than as a team, so neither team is safe. Tyra Sanchez is named the winner and Raven and Mystique were in the bottom. Mystique Summers Madison RuPaul sent home.

Episode Four

The queens are given a mini- challenge called "The Queen is Right," where the girls are shown drag essential items and asked to bid on how much they believe the item is worth. The contestant who comes closest to the actual price wins. Raven wins the challenge. The queens are then asked to impersonate celebrities as part of a "Match Game" homage, called "Snatch Game". Alex Mapa and Phoebe Price are the contestants on the show, and each girl impersonates a different celebrity, with the objective to be as funny as possible within their own character. Jessica Wild impersonated RuPaul. Jujubee impersonated Kimora Lee Simmons. Morgan McMichaeld impersonated Pink. Pandora Boxx impersonated Carol Channing. Raven impersonated Paris Hilton. Sahara Davenport impersonated Whitney Houston. Sonique impersonated Lady Gaga. Tatianna impersonated Britney Spears. And Tyra Sanchez impersonated Beyonce. At the judging panel, the guest judges are Lisa Rinna and Niecy Nash. The challenge winner was Tatianna. The bottom two queens were Morgan McMichaels and Sonique. Sonique RuPaul sent home.

Episode Five

The queens were given a mini challenge to decorate a white box using provided supplies and an item borrowed from another queen, which Raven wins. RuPaul then announces the main challenge of the week. The girls are going to create their very own wedding dress by altering weddings dresses provided to them. As an additional twist to the challenge, the queens will be shooting wedding portraits using not only their girl drag, but their best guy drag as well by posing as both bride and groom for the portraits. At judging the guest judges are Mathu Andersen and Martha Wash. After each contestant poses both as bride and groom for their photos, they then walk the runway in their wedding dress creations. The winner was Tyra Sanchez. The bottom two queens were Morgan McMichaels and Sahara Davenport. Morgan McMichaels RuPaul sent home.

Episode Six

The queens arrive to RuPaul giving them a mini challenge in which they must style a wig, giving it a glam rock makeover. Pandora RuPaul declared winner. RuPaul reveals the remaining contestants a very special and very unique challenge. They must create a rocker chick outfit and perform live vocals to a rock and roll cover to RuPaul's Ladyboy. The queens are given a one-on-one 10 minute rehearsal time with Terri Nunn from the band, Berlin. At the judging panel the guest judges are Terri Nunn and Henry Rollins. The queens performed their rock song for the judges and a small crowd. Jessica Wild RuPaul declared the winner. The bottom two queens were Jujubee and Sahara Davenport. After lip-sync, Sahara Davenport RuPaul sent home.

Episode Seven

The remaining queens were given a mini-challenge where they "read" (insult) the other queens. The queens have no trouble reading each other over anything from physical flaws to personalities. Jujubee wins the mini-challenge. RuPaul then gives the girls their main challenge for the week. Each contestant is to create an autobiography book cover and title that represents their own personal stories about how doing drag has impacted their lives. Jessica Wild's book was called "Jessica Wild: Dreams of a Golden Child. Jujubee's book was called "Memoirs of a Gay-Sha: Jujubee's Journey, I'm Still Here!" Pandora Boxx's book was called "Out of the Boxx: How Drag Saved My Life". Raven's book was called "Young, Broke, and Fabulous: The Pursuit of Finding Your Inner Trust Fund". Tatianna's book was called "Tati: From Teen Queen to Drag Superstar!" And Tyra Sanchez's book was called "The Woman in Me: A Guide to Letting Go of the Past, Accepting the Present, and Looking Forward to a Better Future". As an additional challenge the queen will field questions via a satellite interview, where they must not only present their autobiography, but also promote a new Absolut alcoholic beverage. The guest judges were Gigi Levangie and Jackie Collins. Raven won the challenge. Jessica Wild and Tatianna were the bottom two queens. After lip synching for their lives RuPaul shocked everyone, including Tatianna, by eliminating Jessica Wild from the competition.

Episode Eight

This week's challenges focused entirely on age. For the mini-challenge, the queens had to match all 12 of this season's contestants to their baby pictures, including their own. The main challenge consisted of the girls taking older gay men and transforming them into their drag mothers for the runway. The contestants were also expected to perform a lip synch with their mothers to RuPaul's song "Main Event". After their performances, the girls were judged based on their transformation of their partner into drag queens as well as their lip synch performance. The guest judges were Debbie Reynolds, Cloris Leachman and NYX Comsmetics founder, Toni Ko. Raven won the challenge due to her having the most dramatic makeover out of everyone. Jujubee and Pandora Boxx were in the bottom two. Pandora Boxx was eliminated.

Episode Nine

This week's challenges focused on creating polished looks for different events. For their mini-challenge, the queens had to style and accessorize identical dresses without cutting or gluing them. RuPauls names Tyra Sanchez the mini-challenge winner, and she is placed in charge of choreographing an opening number for "The Diva Awards". The queens must put together three looks for the "The Diva Award" ceremony. "The Teen Diva Awards", where the queens must dress like teen idols. "The Diva DC Press Awards", where the queens must pull out executive realness looks. "The Diva Hollywood Extravaganza Awards", where the queens are expected to wear their most glamarous looks. This guest judges are Tatum O'Neal and Marissa Jaret Winokur. During their opening number, Jujubee misses some of the steps but is praised for keeping poised. Both Raven and Tyra receive high marks for their looks and 'award show speeches. RuPaul names Tyra Sanchez the winner of the challenge. Jujubee and Tatianna are in the bottom two. After lip-sync Tatianna is sent home. The final three is Jujubee, Raven and Tyra Sanchez.

Episode Ten

This is the highlights and outtakes from the second season's first nine episodes. RuPaul shows never-before-seen pre-show audition clips of all the eliminated girls. 'They included Shangela cleaning a car, Nicole Paige Brooks with her son, Mystique explaining her "two-piece and a biscuit", Sonique's outfits and wardrobe, Morgan McMichaels using a back alley as a runway, Sahara Davenport dancing on stage, Jessica speaking about what drag means to her, Pandora's hilarious antics, and Tatianna's sheer femininity. Then season 1 contestants Ongina, Shannel, and season 1 winner BeBe Zahara Benet join RuPaul as she counts down the top ten most unforgettable fits and fashions from the season. After, RuPaul reveals some never-before-seen, behind the scenes moments including the queens impersonating each other, the contestants' family relationships and the unseen moments on the main stage.

Episode Eleven

Merle Ginsberg and Santino Rice arrive to tell the last three queens about their final challenge. Dress in their best 80s outfits and shooting the music video for RuPaul's next single: "Jealous of My Boogie". They will work with guests who include reality star Robert Verdi,who will help the girls with fashion, make-up artist Mathu Anderson, who will direct the video and choreographer Ryan Heffington, who will coach them in a small fight sequence. During the shoot, each girl is given a certain script, where they confront RuPaul and get slapped. At the judging there are no guest judges. It is just RuPaul, Merle Ginsberg, and Santino Rice who will pick the winner. Jujubee is eliminated first. Raven and Tyra Sanchez are left. The two queens must lip synch to "Jealous of My Boogie". RuPaul announces that Tyra Sanchez is the winner of the Season Two, with Raven as runner-up.

Episode Twelve

Season two queens reunite to talk about their journey and The Miss Congeniality Award Winner is announced. Shangela reflects on what happened after (She won the 2010 California Entertainer of the Year award after taping had wrapped). Nicole Paige Brooks reveals that she was disappointed in Raven for talking bad about her when Nicole believed they were friends. Sonique breaks down and then emotionally reveals that she has been unhappy with her life as a queen and so has begun taking hormones to transition from male to female. The second half of contestants come out and Sahara Davenport discusses her family's positive reaction to her drag lifestyle and talks about the fan mail she received. Several of the girls become emotional as Pandora tearfully tells of her father watching the show and calling her to say that he was proud of her just a few weeks before his death. The queens reflect on Tyra's victory and her change to a kinder, quieter demeanor. Tyra reveals she has used some of the prize money to straighten her teeth. RuPaul announces the Miss Congeniality Award, with Pandora Boxx winning in a landslide.

<u>**Season Three**</u>

Episode One

The first episode shows behind the scenes of the casting process for the 2011 edition of "RuPaul's Drag Race." Featured are entrants that were not cast in the series. All the contestants are profiled. Manila's audition tape includes an endorsement from her boyfriend, season 2's Sahara Davenport. Raja reveals she has done make up for some pretty big names in Hollywood and her audition tape includes an endorsement from Adam Lambert. India Ferrah shows us through video and old photos his early drag career which started at 14. Mimi and Stacy were premiered as the Big Girls of the Season. Phoenix talks about her start in drag. Venus D-lite and Delta Work are profiled, and it is revealed that they were chosen as a result of auditioning in front of RuPaul and Santino Rice at an open casting call in Hollywood.

Episode Two

Season Three begins with the introductions of 12 new queens vying to be "the next drag superstar". They are; Alexis Mateo, Carmen Carrera, Delta Work, India Ferrah, Manila Luzon, Mariah, Mimi Imfurst, Phoenix, Raja, Shangela, Stacy Layne Matthews, Venus D-Lite, and Yara Sofia. After the surprise revelation that the first eliminated second-season competitor Shangela has returned to be the thirteenth competitor in season three, the queens receive their first mimi-challenge: a Christmas-card photo shoot on a trampoline with Mike Ruiz taking the pictures. Then it's off to a thrift store to stock up for their holiday-themed runway outfits. The guest judges are Mike Ruiz, Vanessa Williams, and Bruce Vilanch. This season the regular judges are RuPaul, Santino Rice and Michelle Visage who took over from Merle Ginsberg. Raja RuPaul declared the winner of the week. Venus and Shangela land in the bottom two. Venus D-Lite is sent home.

Episode Three

The queens learned that the theme for the week is sci-fi. RuPaul arrives in the workroom to issue the mini-challenge. The queens are asked to pair up with the person they feel they have the strongest psychic connection to (Raja & Delta, Mariah & Phoenix, Carmen & Manila, Alexis & Stacy, Shangela & India and Mimi & Yara) and are then separated by a screen. One team member must "use ESP" to guess the other person's fashion accessories; what color boa, what kind of jewelry, and what color cat. The winning pair is Mariah and Phoenix, with their reward being competing team captains for the main challenge. For the main challenge this week, the girls split into two teams to shoot a trailer for the *Drag Queens in Outer Space* movie saga; the original film, *From Earth to Uranus* (Team Phoenix) and the sequel *Return to Uranus* (Team Mariah). Each team had to shoot a different scene, but with the same characters. This week's guest judges are Lily Tomlin and Alessandra Torresani. Mariah's team won, with Alexis and Shangela sharing the title of the challenge winner and Mimi also receiving praise. Because of two winners that week, no immunity was given. Phoenix and Delta are the bottom two queens. Delta RuPaul declared safe and Phoenix RuPaul sent home.

Episode Four

For their mini-challenge, the queens were asked to create a fashion style using duct tape. In groups of two (and one group of three) the contestants had to glamorize their black leotards using duct tape of various colors. The reward given was competing as team captains for the main challenge. The queens are informed that the main challenge will be two inspirational workout videos. Carmen and Manila are team captains. This week's guest judges are Susan Powter and LaToya Jackson. Billy B filled in for Santio Rice who missed this week. Alexis won the challenge and is given immunity for this win. During lip-sync, Mimi picks up India from in front of the judges table and carries her up to the stage against her will. RuPaul scolds Mimi Imfirst stating, "Drag is not a contact sport!" before eliminating her and declaring India safe.

Episode Five

For the mini-challenges, the queens were given the task of creating a scandalous red carpet photo. The winners became the team leaders as news anchors for "The Morning After News" on fictionalized QNN. To mentor the queens, Debbie Matenopoulos provided tips on personality and delivery. Kristin Cavallari was on hand to be interviewed by the girls as well. Although they worked as team, each member was judged individually. The guest judges are Chloe Sevigny and Debbie Matenopoulos. Billy B was subbing for Santino Rice again. Manila Luzon won the challenge. India Ferrah and Stacy Layne Matthews were in the bottom two. Stacy won lip-sync and India Ferrah RuPaul sent home.

Episode Six

For this week's mini challenge, the queens were asked to play, "S**t RuPaul Says" to win the opportunity to call a family member. Delta won the challenge but gave the prize to Shangela who wanted to speak to her grandmother. The group was then asked to impersonate celebrities on "Snatch Game". The panel was judged by model Amber Rose and Aisha Tyler. Alexis Mateo impersonated Alicia Keys. Carmen Carrera impersonated Jennifer Lopez. Delta Work impersonated Cher. Manila Luzon impersonated Imelda Marcos. Mariah impersonated Joan Crawford. Raja impersonated Tyra Banks. Shangela impersonated Tina Turner. Stacy Layne Matthews impersonated Mo'Nique. Yara Sofia impersonated Amy Winehouse. This week's judges were Aisha Tyler and Amber Rose. For the runway portion, the queens were asked to wear their favorite drag look. Stacy won the challenge. Delta and Mariah "lip-synched for their lives" to remain in the competition. Delta won the lip-sync and Mariah RuPaul sent home.

Episode Seven

At the beginning of the episode, the queens were asked to do a tasteful nude photo shoot with photographer Deborah Anderson. Carmen won the challenge and was given the task to assign each contestant a cake. The main challenge called for a couture fashion ensemble modeled after the assigned cake. Furthermore, each cake had to be decorated to reflect the contestant's personality. This week's judges are Sara Rue and Eliza Dushku. Billy B filed in for an absent Santino Rice. Raja RuPaul declared the winner. Alex Mateo and Stacy Layne Matthews were the bottom two queens. RuPaul decides to keep Alexis Mateo and Stacy Layne Matthews RuPaul sent home. Off stage, a clique begins to form with Raja, Delta, Carmen and Manila referring to themselves as Heathers while Alexis, Yara, Stacy and Shangela were called "boogers".

Episode Eight

In this week's mini-challenge, the cast were asked to "read" each other. Shangela wins the challenge, with her prize being to choose the order of the contestants for the main challenge. RuPaul announces that for the main challenge, the queens have to develop a stand-up comedy routine to perform in front of a live audience. In order to help them put an act together, they each get a one-on-one workshop with legendary comedienne Rita Rudner. Shangela gives the queens the line-up for the show starting with Raja, followed by Carmen, Alexis, Shangela, Manila, Yara and Delta. On the main stage, the contestants debut their comedy routines for the judges and the audience. This week's guest judges are Rita Rudner and Arden Myrin. With Billy B filling in for an absent Santino Rice. Shangela won the challenge. Delta Work and Manila Luzon were the bottom two queens. Manila won lip-sync and Delta Work RuPaul sent home.

Episode Nine

In the mini-challenge, the queens are asked to bedazzle black bras into something spectacular, and Manila wins. The queens are then told they will be making 30-second promos themed around their love of America that will be shown to U.S. military members serving overseas. RuPaul tells the queens to make it personal but entertaining. Each queen comes up with her own strategy. This week's guest judges are Cheryl Tiegs and Johnny Weir. In their runway presentation, the contestants are told to dress in their most patriotic drag. Alexis won the competition for her enthusiastic performance. Carmen Carrera and Yara Sofia were the bottom two queens. Both contestants had to lip sync for their lives but after telling Carmen to stay, RuPaul also told Yara she could stay as well becoming the first non-elimination challenge in the series.

Episode Ten

This week's mini-challenge is a game of "Ru-sical chairs". It is exactly like musical chairs but when the music stops, the chair-less queen must sing the next line in the song. If she gets it she gets to eliminate one of her competitors; if she doesn't, she's out. Manila is the last queen standing. RuPaul announces that the main challenge this week has the queens performing a song for "RuPaul-a-Palooza", and brings out Absolut Vodka spokesman Jeffrey Moran. Each queen is going to record their own version of RuPaul's new song, "Superstar" in one of six distinct musical styles and since Manila won the mini-challenge she gets to pick first and determine the order of the rest of the selections. The queens arrive at the recording studio where they meet Ru's music producer Lucian Piane. The following day the queens find mp3 players with their recorded songs, and all are pleased with the final products except Carmen, who thinks she sounds horrible. This week's guest judges are Jeffrey Moran, Jody Watley, and Carmen Electra. Once again, Santino Rice was absent. Raja was the challenge. Carmen Carrera and Shangela were in the bottom two. Shangela was safe and Carmen Carrera RuPaul sent home.

Episode Eleven

For this week's mini-challenge, the remaining queens were asked to create a fashion-forward, beach themed headpiece with Raja being declared the winner. RuPaul reveals the main challenge: participate in a hair-themed fashion show with three distinct looks. A classic look from another era, a modern red carpet look, and a fantasy hair outfit, which must be made entirely out of wigs. During the episode all of the contestants agreed that this was the hardest challenge so far. This week's judges were Wayne Brady and Fantasia Barrino. Yara Sofia was the challenge. Alexis Mateo and Shangela were the bottom two queens. Alexis Mateo won lip-sync and Shangela RuPaul sent home.

Episode Twelve

As the episode begins, RuPaul reveals that Carmen Carrera is returning to the competition after being unanimously voted back by the other judges. The queens move on to the mini-challenge in which they play RuPaul's version of the dunk tank the Badonkadonk Dunking Machine. Alexis Mateo wins the challenge. RuPaul next announces the main challenge: The queens must make over five masculine heterosexual jocks as their drag sisters. As a twist, RuPaul reveals the queens must also dress their jocks as cheerleaders and perform cheers about safe sex. This week's guest judges were Margaret Cho and Sharon Osbourne. Mike Ruiz was at the judging panel for an absent Santino Rice. The queens and their new drag sisters first perform their safe-sex cheers for the judges and conclude with their runway performances. Manila Luzon won the challenge. Carmen Carrera and Raja were the bottom two queens. Raja is asked to stay and Carmen is once again sent home.

Episode Thirteen

The final four begin this episode with a mini-challenge of creating a marketable drag product from their own wardrobe and then deliver a sales pitch on RuVC. Yara Sofia wins the mini-challenge. RuPaul announces the main challenge to create three looks for three distinct categories: Swimsuit Body Beautiful, Cocktail Attire After 5 and Evening Gown Eleganza, which must be made out of 1 million Ru Dollars. The girls must also perform a choreographed lip-sync to "Just Wanna Dance" by guest judge LaToya Jackson. This week's guest judges were LaToya Jackson and Gigi Levangie Grazer. Mike Riuz was also a judge filling in for an absent Santino Rice. Manila Luzon won the challenge. Alexis Mateo and Yara Sofia were the bottom two queens. During lip-sync the pressures of the competition get to Yara Sofia who completely gives up by shredding her Eleganza look and breaking down crying on stage. Yara Sofia RuPaul sent home.

Episode Fourteen

This episode is a look back at the highlights, low-lights and previously unseen footage from the first 13 episodes. Chaz Bono made a cameo appearance during the episode's opening scene as a cameraman. Season two winner Tyra Sanchez as well as runner-up Raven and Jujubee returned to the provide their opinions on the season's highlights.

Episode Fifteen

The final three return to the workroom where Michelle Visage greets them and delivers the final challenge - costarring in the music video for Ru's song "Champion." The final main stage presentation has the queens in their favorite looks. There were no guest judges this week. After the judges deliberated Alexis Mateo is eliminated from the race. This leaves Manila Luzon and Raja to lip-sync for the crown to RuPaul's "Champion." RuPaul makes her decision declaring Raja the winner. Manila is runner-up.

Episode Sixteen

The queens of RuPaul's Drag Race Season Three reunite for the first time since the shooting of the series. In this reunion special, all thirteen contestants return to give their take on what happened during the show. Plus, the girls confront the judges and each other and RuPaul reveals that Yara Sofia is the winner of the title of Miss Congeniality. One issue brought up was the "Heathers" issue. The four "Heathers" stated they branded themselves this way in fun and did not take it seriously, while many of the other contestants felt that what they did ranged from "stupid" to downright hurtful and took offense to the whole issue.

Season Four

Episode One

Thirteen new queens begin their quests for the title of "America's Next Drag Superstar". This season's queens are; Alisa Summers, Chad Michaels, DiDa Ritz, Jiggly Caliente, Kenya Michaels, Lashauwn Beyond, Latrice Royale, Madame LaQueer, Milan, Phi Phi O'Hara, Sharon Needles, The Princess, and Willam. The queens first mini-challenge is a photo shoot with Mike Ruiz where the queens posed on a spinning platform and sprayed with "toxic waste". For their main challenge, the queens must survive drag zombies and the end of the world that featured some of the queens who have been on the previous seasons. Then the queens must create a look that features a post-apocalyptic world. This week's guest judges were Cassandra Peterson and Mike Ruiz. RuPaul, Michelle Visage and Santino Rice are the regular judges. Sharon Needles won the challenge. Alisa Summers and Jiggly Caliente were the bottom two queens. RuPaul sends Alisa Summers home before declaring Jiggly Caliente as safe.

Episode Two

The queens learn that the next challenge would be a women's wrestling challenge. Further to the mini-challenge, the queens were separated into three teams headed by the mini-challenge winners, and were asked to create a wrestling storyline and to choreograph a match, to be performed in front of the judges and a live audience. In addition, the teams had to split into binomials: the nice girls, or Faces, and the bad girls, or Heels. This week's guest judges were Rick Fox and John Salley. The queens were asked to walk the runway in their best "girly-girl" couture. Team Chad wins the challenge with Chad and Madame being declared the overall winners. The bottom two queens were Lashauwn Beyond and The Princess. The Princes ended up winning lip-sync and Lashuawn Beyond RuPaul sent home.

Episode Three

The queens make commercials for RuPaul's albums "Glamazon" and "Champion". The queens were separated into two teams, led by Phi Phi (team Champion) and Kenya (team Glamazon). The girls were asked to walk the runway with their "platinum and gold" drag looks. This week's guest judges are Amber Riley and Natalie Cole. Sharon Needles won the main challenge. DiDa Ritz and The Princess were in the bottom two. DiDa Ritz won lip-sync and The Princess RuPaul sent home.

Episode Four

At the beginning of the episode, the queens praise DiDa's high-energy lip-sync from the previous episode. For the mini-challenge, the queens are paired up to pose for memorable mug shots. Willam and Madame LaQueer win the mini challenge and the two become team captains for the main challenge: act in a sitcom ("Hot In Tuckahoe") set in a jail. This week's guest judges are Nicole Sullivan and Max Mutchnick. After appearing in their best red carpet attire team Willam RuPaul declared the winning team. Latrice Royale won the main challenge. Madame LaQueer and Milan were the bottom two queens. Milan was told to stay while Madame LaQueen RuPaul sent home.

Episode Five

For the mini-challenge, the queens participate in a game called "Beat the Cock". The winner of the challenge is promised a call home. The main challenge is revealed to be this season's installment of "Snatch Game".   Chad Michaels impersonated Cher. DiDa Ritz impersonated Wendy Williams, Jiggly Caliente impersonated Snooki. Kenya Michaels impersonated Beyonce. Latrice Royale impersonated Aretha Franklin. Milan impersonated Diana Ross. Phi Phi O'Hara impersonated Lady Gaga. Sharon Needles impersonated Michelle Visage. Jiggly Caliente, Phi Phi O'Hara, and Kenya Michaels were openly critiqued by Latrice Royale for their "unprofessional" behavior during the Snatch Game. She scolds them for interrupting RuPaul and the tone of their performances. This week's guest judges are Loretta Devine and Ross Matthews. Chad Michaels is named the winner of the challenge. Kenya Michaels and Milan were the bottom two queens. Milan won lip-sync and Keyna Michaels RuPaul sent home.

Episode Six

The queens learned that for the mini-challenge they would have to do a 'wet t-shirt' contest where the winner would be chosen by the crowds reactions. Willam won the mini-challenge. The queens design ship-shaped floats for a Pride parade runway extravaganza. Each queen representing one color from the rainbow flag for their pride floats. This week's guest judges were Kelly Osbourne and Pauley Perrette. Willam won the challenge. Milan and Jiggly Caliente were the bottom two queens. After lip- sync Jiggy Caliente stayed and Milan RuPaul sent home.

Episode Seven

The queens' mini-challenge was the 'read' challenge where each queen would insult each other. Latrice Royale won the mini-challenge. The queens were then told that they have to come up with a magazine cover for the main challenge. The photo shoot for their magazine cover was with photographer Jonathan Clay Harris. This week's guest judges are Regina King and Pam Tillis. Phi Phi O'Hara RuPaul declared the winner of the challenge. Willam and Jiggly Caliente were the bottom two queens. Willam won lip-sync and Jiggly Caliente RuPaul sent home.

Episode Eight

The queens return to the workroom and find that their mini-challenge is not an actual challenge. Each queen is hooked up to a polygraph machine and given a lie detector test through a series of questions asked by RuPaul. After the questioning, RuPaul reveals the main challenge for the girls: a live performance duet and sing "So Much Better Than You" between two queens who have the least in common with each other, aka "frenemies." The duet partners are Phi Phi O'Hara and Sharon Needles, DiDa Ritz and Chad Michaels, and Latrice Royale and Willam. This week's guest judges were Pamela Anderson and Jennifer Tilly. The winners of the main challenge was Latrice Royale and Willam. Before RuPaul can declare the bottom two Willam, ends up being sick of the side of the stage. Sharon Needles and Phi Phi O'Hara were in the bottom two and had to lip-sync for their lives. After lip-sync RuPaul calls Willam back forward to the stage. RuPaul reveals that Willam has been caught breaking rules lined out in the contract for the show leaving RuPaul no choice but to disqualify Willam and eliminate her from the competition despite her win. Phi Phi and Sharon are then both declared safe in light of this shocking twist.

Episode Nine

The top five queens return to the work room and RuPaul brings them their next mini challenge: create fashionable footwear out of clear platform heels using an Absolut cocktail as inspiration. Phi Phi O'Hara wins the mini-challenge. RuPaul then presents them with their main challenge. The girls will be campaigning for the Drag Queen Presidency and must put together a presentation for a round table political debate. This week's guest judges are Dan Savage and Jeffrey Moran. After deliberation, Sharon Needles RuPaul declared the winner of the challenge. DiDa Ritz and Latrice Royale were the bottom two queens. Latrice Royale won lip-sync and DiDa Ritz RuPaul sent home. However, before the remaining queens could celebrate RuPaul announced one of the eliminated queens will be returning to the competition next week.

Episode Ten

At the start of the episode, the queens begin to wonder which queen would be returning to the competition. Kenya Michaels has returned to the competition and she wins the mini-challenge, which was to drag out a stuffed teddy bear. For their main challenge, the queens are paired up with dads for a maternity runway/makeover and striptease. This week's guest judges are Jesse Tyler Ferguson and Jennifer Love Hewitt. Phi Phi O'Hara was the winner. Kenya Michaels and Latrice Royale is the bottom two queens. Latrice Royale won and was safe. Kenya Michaels RuPaul sent home again.

Episode Eleven

For the mini-challenge, the queens made a puppet of their own peers and made a bitch fest. Chad won the mini-challenge. Chad Michaels pick a each queen and matched a dog to use as inspiration for the main challenge. RuPaul then asked the queens to perform a production number as dogs. "Daytime Dog Park", "Pooch In A Purse", and "Canine Couture Eleganza". This week's guest judges are Rose McGowan and Wynonna Judd. The winner of the challenge is Sharon Needles. Chad Michaels and Latrice Royale were the bottom two queens. Chad Michaels won lip-sync and Latrice Royale RuPaul sent home.

Episode Twelve

This is the episode were we look back on the highlights, low-lights, and previously unseen footage from the season. RuPaul is joined by Shannel (season 1), Pandora Boxx (season 2) and Mariah (season 3) as they look back over the top 10 fits of fashion from the season so far.

Episode Thirteen

The queens compete in their final challenge starring in RuPaul's music video for "Glamazon". Candis Cayne helped them to their choreography. This week's guest judges were Candis Cayne and Mathu Anderson. In a twist all three finalists had to perform lip-sync song. Afterwards, RuPaul announced that the winner of the race will be revealed on "RuPaul's Drag Race: Reunited" the next week and after asking fans to share their opinions with her on Twitter and Facebook© to help her decide on the winning queen.

Episode Fourteen

For the first time a live audience of fans sit in as RuPaul and the contestants return for the annual reunion where RuPaul reveals the winner of the season. We find out Latrice Royale is crowned "Miss Congeniality." We also learn that the reason Willam was disqualified was that he was caught having conjugal visits with his husband. The queen who won RuPaul's Drag Race season 4 was Sharon Needles.

Season Five

Episode One

This season's fourteen new queens are Alaska, Alyssa Edwards, Coco Montrese, Detox, Honey Mahogany, Ivy Winters, Jade Jolie, Jinkx Monsoon, Lineysha Sparx, Monica Beverly Hillz, Penny Tration, Roxxxy Andrews, Serena Cha Cha, and Vivienne Pinay. For the first mini-challenge the queens had to do an underwater photo shoot with Mike Ruiz. Detox is the winner of the mini-challenge. RuPaul announces for the main challenge the queens will need to construct a 'Hollywood Glamor' outfit made from materials salvaged from a dumpster in Beverly Hills. This week's guest judges are Camille Grammer and Mike Ruiz. RuPaul, Michelle Visage, and Santino Rice are the regular judges. Roxxxy Andrews wins the challengePenny Tration and Serena ChaCha end up as the bottom two queens. Serena ChaCha RuPaul saved and Penny Tration RuPaul sent home. A rivalry between two contestants emerged between Alyssa Edwards and Coco Montrese. The two queens competed in the Miss Gay American competition back in 2010. The rivalry between both queens came from the fact that Alyssa was disqualified from a competition after being crowned replaced by Coco, the runner-up, taking her crown.

Episode Two

The queens mini-challenge consisted of lip-synching one of three of RuPaul's songs; "Tanny Chaser", "Lady Boy", or "Peanut Butter" with only their mouth visible. The winners were Serena ChaCha, Detox, and Ivy Winters. The three winners became team captains for the main challenge. The main challenge was to impersonate memorable scenes from RuPaul's Drag Race Untucked. This week's guest judges were Juliette Lewis and Kristen Johnston. After viewing each team's clip RuPaul announces team Ivy Winters is the winning team with Lineysha Sparx declared the winner of the challenge. During the critiques Monica Beverly Hillz reveales that is a transgendered woman. The bottom two queens were Monica Beverly Hillz and Serena ChaCha. Monica Beverly Hillz won lip-sync and Serena ChaCha RuPaul sent home.

Episode Three

The queens learn that the mini-challenge each queens are paired-up with another queen and had to take a blank mannequin doll and create a mini-pageant for "America's Junior Drag Superstar". Alaska and Lineysha Sparx paired up together and were the winner of the mini-challenge. For the main challenge, the queens had to create a kid TV-show. As winners of the mini-challenge, Alaska and Lineysha were team captains. For their main runway look, the contestants had to dress in pink. This week's guest judges were Coco Austin and Pauline Porizkova. Detox RuPaul declared the winner. Coco Montrese and Monica Beverly Hillz were the bottom two queens. Coco Montrese outshined Monica Beverly Hillz in lip synch and RuPaul saved. Monica Beverly Hillz RuPaul sent home.

Episode Four

For this episode's mini-challenge, the queens had to participate in a dance-off dancing to "Jealous of My Boogie". RuPaul chose Jinkx Monsoon and Coco Montrese as the winners of the mini-challenge and became team captains for the main challenge. This week the queens are challenged to prove their elegance and dancing skills by starring in a ballet based on the life of RuPaul. This week's guest judges are Chaz Bono and Travis Wall. Alyssa Edwards' dancing and her characterization of 'Bad RuPaul' secure her the win. RuPaul names Vivienne Pinay and Honey Mahogany as the bottom two queens. After a fairly low-key lip synch RuPaul surprises everyone by eliminating both queens. This was the first in the history of RuPaul's Drag Race that two queens RuPaul eliminated on the same episode.

Episode Five

The queens compete in a star-studded TV game show that highlights their celebrity impersonations the "Snatch Game". Alaska impersonated Lady Bunny. Alyssa Edwards impersonated Katy Perry. Coco Montrese impersonated Janet Jackson. Detox impersonated Ke$ha. Ivy Winters impersonated Marilyn Monroe. Jade Jolie impersonated Taylor Swift. Jinx Monsoon impersonated Little Edie. Lineysha Sparkx impersonated Celia Cruz. Roxxxy Andrews impersonated Tamar Braxton. This week's guest judges were Julie Brown and Downtown Julie Brown. The main challenge winner was Jinkx Monsoon. The bottom two queens were Detox and Lineysha Sparx. Detox's unique style during lip-syncing kept her in the competition. Lineysha Sparx RuPaul sent home.

Episode Six

For the queens mini-challenge is the queens were given the task to apply make-up in the dark. RuPaul declared Detox the winner. For the main-challenge, the queens had record a "We Are The World" inspired charity single. For this week's mainstage look, RuPaul wanted the queens to have an outfit that showcased their best body part. This week's guesd judges were LaToya Jackson and The Pointer Sisters, Anita Pointer and Ruth Pointer. Ivy Winters was the winner of this week's main challenge. Jade Jolie and Coco Montrese landed in the bottom two queens. Coco Montrese won lip-sync and Jade Jolie RuPaul sent home.

Episode Seven

For this week's mini-challenge, the queens were asked to "read" the other contestants. RuPaul declared Alaska the winner of the mini-challenge. For the main challenge, the contestants had to roast RuPaulin front of a live audience. As winner of the mini-challenge, Alaska decided the order in which the queens would perform. Nadya Ginsburg, Deven Green, and Bruce Vilanch coached the queens and guided them for their live performance. This week's guest judges were Leslie Jordan and Jeffrey Moran. Coco Montrese RuPaul declared the winner of the main challenge. Roxxxy Andrews and Alyssa Edwards landed in the bottom two. RuPaul decided to give both queens another chance and they were both safe.

Episode Eight

This week's mini-challenge had the queens play Drag Race's version of the memory game. After all the queens completed the challenge Ivy Winters RuPaul declared winner. RuPaul announced that the main-challenge of this week would be to create, market, and film a commercial for a signature fragrance. This week's guest judges were Aubrey O'Day and Joan Van Ark. Alaska was the winner of this challenge. Ivy Winters and Alyssa Edwards landed in the bottom two. After their lip-synch performance RuPaul told Alyssa Edwards to stay and Ivy Winters RuPaul sent home.

Episode Nine

During the mini-challenge of this week, the queens had to cry on cue as RuPaul asked the contestants to create a fake sob story and cry. After the mini-challenge was over RuPaul declared Detox and Alyssa Edwards winners. For this week's main challenge the queens had to star in a Latin telenovela with co-star Wilmer Valderrama. As winners of the mini-challenge, Alyssa Edwards and Detox picked the teams. This week's guest judges were Maria Conchita Alonso and Jamie-Lynn Sigler. For the runway presentation, RuPaul asked the queens to be dressed in their best Latin glamor. Jinkx Monsoon RuPaul declared the winner. Alyssa Edwards and Coco Montrese were asked to lip-synch for their lives. After the performance by both queens Coco Montrese could stay in the competition and Alyssa Edwards RuPaul sent home.

Episode Ten

For the mini-challenge, the remaining queens were exposed to drag boot camp by Storm a fitness trainer. Alaska won the challenge for outlasting the other queens. Alaska got to match the queens to a gay veteran for a drag makeover. This week's guest judges were Clinton Kelly and George Kotsiopoulos. On the main stage, the queens and veterans were challenged to perform a patriotic flag salute before walking the runway displaying their transformation. Roxxxy Andrews won the challenge while Coco Montrese and Detox lip-synched for their lives. Detox won lip-sync and Coco Montrese RuPaul sent home.

Episode Eleven

This week's mini-challenge the queens had to make a puppet of their own peers and made a "bitch fest" of which Alaska RuPaul declared the winner. For the main challenge, the queens had to participate in the Sugar Ball and design three outfits in three different categories: "Super Duper Sweet 16", "Sugar Mama-Executive Realness", and "Candy Couture". As the winner of the mini-challenge Alaska was given the tasked with choreographing a dance routine for all four queens as an opening number to a song. This week's guest judges were Marg Helgenberger and Bob Mackie. Alaska won the challenge. Jinkx Monsoon and Detox ended up in the bottom two. After a well performed lip-synch by both queens, RuPaul allowed Jinkx Monsoon to stay and Detox RuPaul sent home.

Episode Twelve

This week Michelle Visage came to announce the week's main challenge to the queens. The main challenge consisted of two parts: star in RuPaul's music video "The Beginning" and shooting a dramatic courtroom scene. For the music video, the queens had to learn a choreography by Candis Cayne. Then for the courtroom scene, each queens had to portray three different roles: the defense attorney, the defendant, and the prosecutor. Mathu Anderson was directing the queens during the scenes. During the final runway presentation, no guest judges were present only Michelle Visage, Santino Rice and RuPaul. Like previous season RuPaul announced that she did not made up her mind and that she would need the help of the public to decide who "America's Next Drag Superstar" will be and is going to be announced during the reunion episode.

Episode Thirteen

This is the episode where we take a look back on the highlights, low-lights, and previously unseen footage from the season as we race toward the climactic crowning of America's Next Drag Superstar. With guest appearances by Latrice Royale, Willam, and Sharon Needles.

Episode Fourteen

Wigs fly as the queens discuss the drama of the season. Plus, both "America's Next Drag Superstar" and "Miss Congeniality" are crowned. Ivy Winters is crowned "Miss Congeniality". The winner for RuPaul's Drag Race Season 5 was Jinx Monsoon.

SHOW TWO OF THREE: All Stars Season

Episode One

This season twelve queens from the previous seasons, returned to compete as an "All Star". The queens who came back were; Alexis Mateo, Chad Michaels, Jujubee, Latrice Royale, Manila Luzon, Mimi Imfurst, Nina Flowers, Pandora Boxx, Raven, Tammie Brown, Shannel, and Yara Sofia. The twelve returning queens are surprised to learn they will be competing in teams of two and that both team members will be eliminated together. The first challenge is for the teammates to make each other up for a high fashion photo shoot. In the first picture, "Half-baked", the queens are to show themselves in the process of being made-up, with no wigs. For "Opposites Attract" the queens have to portray a concept that conveys opposites. This week's guest judges were Rachel Hunter and Ross Matthews. Returning as the regular judges are Michelle Visage, Santino Rice, and RuPaul. Team Latrila (Latrice Royale and Manlia Luzon) wins the challenge. After deliberation, Team Shad (Shannel and Chad Michaels) and Team Mandora (Mimi Imfurst and Pandora Boxx) find themselves the bottom two teams. Mimi Imfurst and Chad Michaels were chosen to lip synch. Chad wins and Team Shad stays while Pandora Boxx and Mimi Imfurst are eliminated.

Episode Two

The mini-challenge, "In Da Butt Ru" tests how well the teams know each other by asking them questions in the style of "The Newlywed Game". For the main challenge, the teams had to write original comedy material for a "Laugh-In" style sketch show. For the show, the queens delivered celebrity impersonations. Team Brown Flowers; Tammie Brown impersonated Tammie Faye Messner and Nina Flowers impersonated La Lupe. Team Latrila; Latrice Royale impersonated Oprah Winfrey and Manila Luzon impersonated Madonna. Team Rujubee; Raven impersonated Bea Arthur and Jujubee impersonated Fran Drescher. Team Shad; Shannel impersonated Lucille Ball and Chad Michaels impersonated Bette Davis. Team Yarlexis; Yara Sofia impersonated Charo and Alexis Mateo impersonated Shakira. Each team had to perform three segments; a cocktail party, a joke exchange with RuPaul and a joke wall. For the runway, teams displayed their best 1960s fashions.This week's guest judges were Busy Phillips and Vicki Lawrence. Team Yarlexis (Yara Sofia and Alexis Mateo) won the challenge. While Team Latrilla and Team Brown Flowers were the bottom two teams. Latrice Royale and Tammie Brown lip-synced to "There's No Business Like Show Business". Latrice Royale won lip-sync and Team Latrila (Latrice Royale and Manila Luzon) stayed. Team Brown Flowers (Tammie Brown and Nina Flowers) RuPaul sent home.

Episode Three

In the mini-challenge, the queens had to take a photograph posed as a sexy macho male. Team Yarlexis (Yara Sofia and Alex Mateo) won. For the main challenge, each queen under the direction of their partner via earpiece had to go to Hollywood Boulevard and convince passers-by to participate in pranks. On the runway, the queens were to wear "girl gone bad" outfits.This week's guest judges were Rachel Dratch and Janice Dickinson. Team Shad (Shannel and Chad Michaels) won the challenge. Team Latrila (Latrice and Manila Luzon) and Team Rujubee (Raven and Jujubee) are declared the bottom two. Manila Luzon and Jujubee perform lip-sync. Jujubee won lip sync and Team Rujubee stayed while Team Latrila (Latrice Royale and Manila Luzon) were sent home.

Episode Four

In the mini challenge the girls had to dress up in cheer-leading costumes and "read" the other contestants in a cheer format. Team Yarlexis (Yara Sofia and Alexis Mateo) were the winners of this mini challenge. The main challenge was to form a girl group with celebrity women and drag them up into a Drag Girl Group. Team Yarlexis (Yara Sofia and Alexis Mateo) selected Kelly Osbourne daughter of Ozzy and Sharon Osbourne. Team Shad (Shannel and Chad Michaels) selected Jillian Hervey, Vanessa Williams' daughter. Team Rujubee (Raven and Jujubee) selected Katy Z, Pia Zadora's daughter. This week's guest judges were Mary Wilson and Rosie Perez. Once again, Team Shad (Shannel and Chard Michaels) wins the challenge. Team Rujubee (Raven and Jujubee) and Team Yarlexis (Yara Sofia and Alexis Mateo) were the bottom two teams. Raven and Alexis Mateo were the original performers of lip-sync but within a minute after the start of the performance Yara Sofia hits the she-mergency button and tags Alexis to finish lip-sync. Raven wins lip-sync for Team Rujubee and Team Yarlexis RuPaul sent home.

Episode Five

In the mini challenge, the remaining pairs played a basketball mini-challenge. Team Rujubee (Raven and Jujubee) won. For the main challenge the teams created a story about a Super Hero and a Super Villain. Chad and Jujubee play their teams' superheroes, while Raven and Shannel play the villains. This week's guest judges were Wendi McClendon-Lovey and Elvira. Team Shad (Shannel and Chad Michaels) won for a third straight week in a row. Team Rujubee (Raven and Jujubee) lip- synced for their lives for the third straight week as well. This time Raven and Jujubee must lip-sync against each other. After an emotional lip-sync, RuPaul elected to save both of the queens and advance them to the finale and for first time in Drag Race history to have a "final four" instead of a final three.

Episode Six

For their final challenge the final queens have to go to different locations within minutes of each other and perform different shows, consisting of a group interview, followed by an appearance at Hamburger Mary's to accept an award in their honor, and finish up with a comedy routine in front of a live audience. The queens, now competing as individuals, were then divided into pairs to attend the events. Chad Michaels and Raven were teamed to leave with season one's Ongina in her car. Jujubee and Shannel were teamed to leave with season three's Delta Work in her car. This week's guest judges were Beth Ditto and Cheri Oteri. After deliberating for the last time this season RuPaul eliminates Jujubee and Shannel leaving Chad and Raven to lip-sync for the final time. Chad Michaels was crowned as the winner of RuPaul's All-Star Drag Race and the first inductee into Drag Race Hall of Fame.

SHOW THREE OF THREE: DragU

RuPaul's Drag U premise is having three normal women get drag makeovers. They are taught to bring out their inner divas. Each of the three women are judged by the 'drag transformation', 'performance', and 'attitude adjustment' (DPA). The contestant with the highest DPA wins. RuPaul is the "President" of Drag U. Unlike in *RuPaul's Drag Race*, he does not appear in drag. Regular judges in season one were "Dean of Drag" Lady Bunny and "Dean of Dance" Frank Gatson, Jr.. For season two, Lady Bunny returned as "Dean of Drag", and various choreographers rotated throughout the season as "Deans of Dance". Each episode features one celebrity guest judge who is usually female. The "Professors" at Drag U were; Alexis Mateo, BeBe Zarhara Benet, Carmen Carrera, Chad Michaels, Delta Work, Jujubee, Latrice Royale, Manila Luzon, Mariah, Morgan McMichaels, Nina Flowers, Ongina, Pandora Boxx, Raja, Raven, Shannel, Sharon Needles, Tammie Brown, Tyra Sanchez, and Willam.

Season 1

The episodes start with RuPaul introducing three "students" to their assigned drag professors for each episode. The students meet RuPaul and then asks them to "walk this way" to the Drag Lab. The students then meet their professors who ask them some intimate questions and try to find out what has brought them to Drag U. RuPaul presents each student with their "Dragulator" image and name.

Each episode includes an "extra credit" game in which students can earn a special prize. They then take part in a dance lesson with the Dean Of Dance to learn the choreography for their performance. On "Draguation Day", the women strut their stuff on the runway perform their designated song and dance routine, and get graded by the judges on the DPA. The student with the highest DPA wins and is presented with a diploma and feather boa from her drag professor.

Season 2

Some of the changes has the former extra credit part of the show and is replaced with "Lady Lessons" taught personally by Lady Bunny. The ladies attend a dance class taught by new Deans of Dance and then proceed to the newly renovated drag lab, where the women work with their drag professors on their new image. The next day, "Draguation Day", has each professor introducing their student to friends and family. The ladies strut on the runway and perform for the audience. Students no longer receive letter grades but instead are sent backstage to the green room as the judges deliberate and decide on a winner. RuPaul is present, but does not influence the vote nor take part in it. RuPaul announces the winner and the winner's professor gives her diploma and a feather boa in the university's colors of purple and orange.

Season 3

In the third season of Drag U, Rupaul's segment "A Word From Rupaul" was altered to include definitions of the word. "Drag Tips" continued, featuring a new professor each week, and Lady Bunny continued to host "Lady Lessons". In May of 2013 RuPaul announced that the series had been canceled.

The World's Largest Printed Directory for Male and Female Impersonators

DRAG411 mails The Forum twice a year to all participating LGBT-friendly show bars and venues in 32 countries. It is available in over 14,000 retailers around the world to benefit HIV/AIDS families.

To place a listing in the July through December 2014 edition:

Discounted 2014 prices

40-word listing with no photo: Was $19.99 / **Now $9.99**
41 to 120-word listing with no photo: Was $24.99 / Now $14.99
40-word listing with small photo: Was $29.99 / Now $19.99
41 to 120-word listing with small photo: Was $34.99 / Now $24.99
Quarter page display listing: Was $79.99 / Now $49.99
Half-page display listing: Was $99.99 / Now $69.99
Full-page display advertisement: Was $159.99 / Now $129.99

Admin@DRAG411.com

NOTE: We are offering the discount to pack out the holiday issues of this book, when venues are hiring the most, people are exchanging this book as gifts, and the book season is in full swing around the world. Drag411 does not edit content in THE FORUM. All content posted exactly as it is sent to us.

Alphabetical; enabling you to check everyone out equally.

6S Boutique
Retailer
        6S Boutique "A Stage Performer's Boutique" KRYOLAN, La Femme, Lashes, Tights & Much More!!!{LGBT Owned & Operated} 6sboutique.com

A Stych in Tyme
Costumers
        A Stych in Tyme has been providing "Custom Clothing at Reasonable Prices" since 2003. Always LGBT friendly; specializing in corsets and Drag costumes.

Aasha Fierce
Queen

Charismatic Female Impersonator and Entertainer, Miss Aasha Fierce. To book or contact me, send an email to aasha72279@gmail.com or friend me at Facebook.com/aasha.feirce

AJ Menendez
Male Illusionist

I've been a Male Illusionist since 2008 and have respect for the craft. Current Titles: Master Male Illusionist, Mister Boiling Point, Mister St. Augustine Pride 2012, Mister Rainbow Hours 2012   For booking information, I can be contacted via Facebook© or @ AJMenendez69@gmail.com

Alexandria Bellterra
Female impersonator

Young, beautiful, energetic, entertainer with so much to offer. Located in the Dayton area and willing to travel, Book today through facebook©.

Alisa Summers
Female impersonator

For Booking Information and Details Contact:
All Starr Management Office: (678) 383-9902
Email: AllStarrManagement@gmail.com
allstarrmanagement.com

**100% of The Advertisements
sold in this magazine were
donated to
The Joshua Tree Feeding Program.
A program feeding HIV families**

Amy DeMilo

Miss Gay USofA Classic 2013.
Show director at the Honey Pot Ybor
City, drag queen bingo hostess at
Hamburger Mary's Tampa. Google,
YouTube, or Facebook ©Amy DeMilo

Anson Reign

Male impersonator
        Anson Reign has won awards
in Arizona, Arkansas, Nebraska, and
more and has performed as an MI
across the country since 2008. He is
the founder & director of Kings for
a Cause - A National Drag Event.

Apollo's Lounge

<Advertisement on page 24.>
Night Bar / Show venue
        Address: 5749 N 7th St, Phoenix,
AZ 85014 Phone: (602) 277-9373 Hours:
Daily 10:00 am – 2:00 am
facebook.com/apollos.phoenix`

Arizona Gender Outlaws

        Cult Leader, Pandora DeStrange,
first gathered together this group of rebellious
queens to Teach Tolerance through Terrorism.
They would get dressed in drag and hit the streets armed only with a camera, razor
sharp wit and the intention to connect with others and bring some well needed fun
into their dreary lives of the people they encountered. After all…"Sometimes it just
takes a fairy" and there are a lot of uptight people in the desert that could use a
laugh. Their antics were often well received by the community. People seemed to
appreciate these playful queens and the joy they seemed to emulate to those they
connected with. They visited the Light Rail, Tempe Town Lake and most notably
Mesa's Fiesta Mall…where they were consequently kicked out and banned for a
year. Not wanting to miss an opportunity to enlighten the masses to the joys of
drag, these queens returned to Fiesta Mall a year later with a about 30 of their
friends and declared July 5th Drag Independence Day by performing The Age of
Aquarius in the Center of the Mall! They were a Huge Hit! They connected with a
lovely family who were struggling with raising a transgender child and they were
able to give them resources and some well needed encouragement. This time they
weren't kicked out either…although they did turn off the escalator (as if drag
queens can run up an escalator in 6 inch heels!!!) Drag Terrorism Success!

Pandora DeStrange and the Arizona Gender Outlaws produce several award winning shows in The Valley of the Sun including Snatch...an Act of Drag Terrorism, The VooDoo Revue, The Follies....NOT Your Typical Drag Show and Dirty Disney to name a few. They can be found performing all over this great nation! If you would like for them to bring a Taste of Drag Terrorism to Your Town then simply contact Pandora DeStrange directly pandoradestrange@gmail.com. The Amazing Jennifer Tristan of 61 Productions compiled their antics on a 2 DVD Set called Drag Terrorism and Other Oddities which can be purchased by contacting her directly at 61productions.com. Also be sure to check out their Videos on YouTube at youtube.com/JLTristan . Remember..."When Freedom is Outlawed, Only Outlaws will be FREE"!

ATTENTION: Did you know you can post your free photo of yourself in face on the DRAG411 Facebook© page? We will place it in the official album, tag you so you can watch people around the world compliment you, and even post your own booking information under the album listing. Most of the famous kings and queens are active on the page.

Ariel Gibbs
Female impersonator
    Available for your booking
needs by writing missamg37@aol.com

BecHavn Publishing
Publisher
    Your boutique publisher creating
autobiographies, historical books, resource
guides, and novels. BecHavn.com

BoomBoom LaRue's
Business
    Serving the Diversity of our
Community

Brandon K. Young-Taylor
Male Illusionist
    As one of the most traveled
Male Illusionist in the US. Brandon
is always looking to hit the next
stage!! To book him at your show
email: BrandonYoungMI@aol.com.

Bebe Zahara Benet
Female impersonator
BeBe Zahara Benet from Cameroon
and winner of the title of "America's Next Drag
Superstar" from the first season of the popular
reality television series RuPaul's Drag Race.
For Booking Information and Details
Contact: All Starr Management
Office: (678) 383-9902
Email: AllStarrManagement@gmail.com
allstarrmanagement.com

BS West
Night Bar / Show venue
Address: 7125 E 5th Ave, Scottsdale, AZ 85251
Phone: (480) 945-9028
Hours: Daily 2:00 pm – 2:00 am

Chase N Yu
Male Illusionist

Candi Samples,
The Peoples Empress ICSD Imperial Court De
San Diego
        I am the reigning Empress of - San Diego
the Peoples Empress ICSD Imperial Court De
San Diego. for over 40 years of noble deeds
Imperialcourtsandiego.com or visit my site
Empresscandisamples.comThe Queen Mother
live here in SD We just lost our founder of the Court system a couple months ago.
Mother Jose
Sarria in 1965 she proclaimed herself the Empress of San Francisco and lead the
foundation fr the I.C. there are over 65 chapters.

Ceceilia Grace Damarco O'Deria
Female impersonator
        I am a drag queen in New Hampshire. I travel to Lowell Massachusetts. I
have performed at club 313 and blue shamrock. I love to perform for audience and
put smiles one faces. Contact ceceiliagrace11@gmail.com

Champagne T. Bordeaux
Female impersonator
        For Booking Information and
Details Contact:
All Starr Management Office: (678) 383-9902
Email: AllStarrManagement@gmail.com
allstarrmanagement.com

Daphne Ferraro

Daphne Ferraro is the show hostess and show director at Hamburger Mary's (Ybor City) on Friday nights. She is the current reigning Miss Large and Lovely National and the creator of several original productions. She is known as the "Tallest Queen in Captivity" and is known for her extreme creativity and unique sense of humor.

Dee Gregory

Dee Gregory a gender illusionist in Jacksonville, FL. Known for Broadway, show tunes, and comedy numbers, Dee loves the spotlight, especially when it is in help of other entertainers and especially charitable organizations.

Dida Ritz

Female impersonator
        For Booking Information and Details Contact:
All Starr Management Office:
(678) 383-9902
Email: AllStarrManagement@gmail.com
allstarrmanagement.com

Divine Decadence Darling

Retail

2393 Agricola at. Halifax, gay owned and operated jewelry and gift store. Amazing bling pieces. We offer 20% off to all glbt customers. Tax included in our prices coming soon Miss Divine Decadence....

Dove

Female impersonator

The Dove of Kansas City is available for booking at Dashingdove79@hotmail.com

(sic) Latin adverb: ("thus"; in full: sic erat scriptum, "thus was it written." Indicates DRAG411 transcribed the comments into this book as found in the original source, complete with any erroneous or archaic spelling or other nonstandard presentation. We try to print the responses using the same words sent to us, ensuring the reader DRAG411 did not change the tone, reflection, or character of each response.

Drag Queen Trolley Follies
        Take a 90-minute tour of downtown Sarasota. $20.00 bring your own drinks in a small cooler we pick up and drop off from the Palm Avenue garage downtown Sarasota. Visit our website dragqueentrolleyfollies.com

Dragqueenwigs.com
        "Amsterdam's" Queen's Hairdresser. My hairstyles come from the heart!!!

Dupree's Discount Drag Supplies
www.dupreesdiscountdrag.com

Eileen Dover
        Minneapolis, MN based performer who has 18 years' experience that includes performing in 19 states, winning 14 pageant titles, competing in eight national pageants.

Mona Regina Alexandria Lee, Empress of Vancouver II
        Empress 2 of Vancouver, B.C. Canada, Empress 5 of Victoria B.C. 1976, Imperial Grand Czarina to the Empress of Canada Foundation, Board of the Imperial Court of the Peace Arch. Surrey, B.C. Canada.

Francina Holliday
Queen: FIERCE!!!!

Freddy Prinze Charming
Male Illusionist
Freddy Prinze Charming has been entertaining audience since 2006. He is the most award winning drag king in Arizona, winning well over a dozen awards and titles.
www.freddyprinzecharming.com
Photo by Gabe King

Gage Gatlyn
Male Illusionist

Known throughout the King community for: "Raising the Bar" by exposing a new kind of 'kinging'; encouraging more realistic use of facial hair, concealment of binding, packing, contouring, and MORE. He was first King booked in over 100 venues Nationwide.

Gilda Golden
Author / Female Impersonator

Check out my book, "Life Outside the Line," available through thousands of retailers around the world.

GSHRadio.com
Internet Radio Station

GSHRadio.com is The Voice and Beat for the GLBT Community. Broadcasting 24/7 with hit music and broadcasting live from the Flamingo Resort! Hope you can tune is as we're tuned into you! www.gshradio.com

Hamburger Mary's
<Clearwater and Tampa advertisement on page thirteen.>
Clearwater: Open Daily Sunday - Thursday 11am to 11pm, Friday & Saturday 11am to 2am, 28910 US Hwy 19 North, Clearwater, FL 33761 Ph (727) 400-6996
Jacksonville : Open Daily 11:00am - 1:30am (Kitchen "last call" at 12:30am). 3333 Beach Blvd. Jacksonville, FL 32207. Ph (904) 551-2048
Orlando: OPEN Daily at 11am Happy Hour Monday – Friday 2pm to 5pm and 10pm to Close. Brunch served Sundays until 3:00pm. 110 West Church St. Orlando, FL 32801 Ph (321) 319-0600 Fax (321) 319-0601
Tampa: Open Daily Monday - Thursday 11am to 11pm, Friday & Saturday 11am to 1am, Sunday 11am to 9pm, 1600 E 7th Ave., 2nd Floor Tampa, FL 33605 Ph (813) 241-6279

Palm Springs : Open Daily Monday - Friday 11am to closing, Saturday & Sunday 10am to closing. Happy Hour 4pm to 6pm. 415 N Palm Canyon Drive Palm Springs, CA 92262 Ph (760) 778-MARY (6279)

Honey Pot
> Address: 1507 E 7th Ave, Tampa, FL 33605 Phone:(813) 247-4663

Jada
> Real world of freezone u now since I been I las vegas nv I do drag at free zone real world of drag there its down to earth real place to be on Wednesday and Friday night sat night for fun real ppl come see detox diva and cast they now how to party hard request jada winters to here now I'm there to entertainment it free.

Jen Menace
Promoter
> Jen Menace - Drag Promoter, DJ, King Manager, and Show Director. Contact @ jenmenace@gmail.com

Jade Jolie
Female impersonator
> For Booking Information and Details
Contact: All Starr Management Office: (678) 383-9902
Email: AllStarrManagement@gmail.com
allstarrmanagement.com

(sic) Latin adverb: ("thus"; in full: sic erat scriptum, "thus was it written." Indicates DRAG411 transcribed the comments into this book as found in the original source, complete with any erroneous or archaic spelling or other nonstandard presentation. We try to print the responses using the same words sent to us, ensuring the reader DRAG411 did not change the tone, reflection, or character of each response.

Jade Sotomayor
Female impersonator

Jade or Jade Chicago born (David Sotomayor) is a Drag Queen, dancer, model and makeup artist from Chicago, Illinois. Jade was in the cast of the first RuPaul's Drag Race. For Booking Information and Details Contact: All Starr Management Office: (678) 383-9902
Email: AllStarrManagement@gmail.com
allstarrmanagement.com

Jocelyn Summers
Female impersonator

For Booking Information and Details
Contact: All Starr Management Office: (678) 383-9902
Email: AllStarrManagement@gmail.com
allstarrmanagement.com

Joe Posa
Female impersonator

Actor, Dancer, Comedian and Female Impersonator, Joe began as a dancer at the age of six, went on to study acting at the American Academy of Dramatic Arts in NYC, and then later launched his career as one of the top character impersonators in the US. As a long standing member of Actor's Equity and SAG, his credits include the International touring company of "West Side Story", "A Chorus Line", " Grease", "The Music Man" , "Anything Goes" and "Joseph and the Amazing Technicolor Dreamcoat". His television appearances include, "Law & Order", "NYPD Blue", " The Sopranos", "Sex and the City", "All My Children", 30 Rock, "Late Night with Conan O'Brien", "Geraldo "and ABC's "The Next Best Thing". Joe also appeared in such movies as "Scent of a Woman", "Carlito's Way", "The Pelican Brief", "The Associate", and "The Mirror Has Two Faces" with Barbra Streisand! Fabulous dancer and later achieving success as a musical theater performer, Joe's gift as an Impersonator has brought him critical acclaim, appearing with many of the Divas he impersonates. Whether appearing in casinos, nightclubs, or an intimate cabaret setting, he knows how to captivate a crowd! For Booking Information and Details Contact: All Starr Management Office: (678) 383-9902 Email: AllStarrManagement@gmail.com allstarrmanagement.com

Joey Brooks
Female Impersonator, Show director, hostess, author…

"Old school, new school, no school … who gives a shit?"
 I'm too old to go to school. I barely remember last week. When I get too old to remember what the fuck I did when I was young …ger, I'll just open of these books and laugh my ass off. I wonder how many other queens had this much fun becoming one of the icons of their community. Too funny. I just called myself an icon. Hell, I must be a queen. Only a female impersonator could call themselves a diva, a queen, a star without people giggling behind her back. Giggling is good. A twenty-dollar bill is better. <You can order my damn book from thousands of retailers to directly from MillionHugs.com.>

K.C. Pettit
        K.C. Pettit is a Classic King performing in the Central Arizona area. He has his head firmly in the 90's and a love of camp.

KaChina Rave
Queen
        Open stage & work my way up minded Drag Entertainer.

Kamden T. Rage
Drag Queen / Entertainer
I am a Native American Vegatarian Virgo who loves the Meat! Love Entertaining with my array of characters ranging from Annie Lennox, P!nk, Marilyn Manson, Mad Hatter, and MANY MORE!! I also love helping my COMMUNITY by doing Benefits and Charities! I am also VERY active in my Community by helping out various organizations from the BEAR & LEATHER Community to Gay-Straight Alliances!

Kameo DuPree
Kameo Dupree is a male illusionist coming out of St. Louis, MO. Kameo can be contacted @ 314-260-9103 and is available for all engagements (day or night)

Katarina Alexander Archer
The Blazing Emerald and Diamond Heart Empress of Eternal Love & Friendship

Kathey Action Tyme Success
Drag Show Promoter.
A FAN of CoCo Montrese, and RuPaul. I LOVE the Fine Arts of Drag, LGBT Community, and Pageantry. Strive for HiV/Aids Awareness. Mailing Address: Kathey Action Tyme Success 462 Wilkinson Rd NE Ludowici, GA 31316 Phone: (678)-607-6103

Kelly Mantle
Female Impersonator
For Booking Information and Details Contact:
All Starr Management Office: (678) 383-9902
Email:
AllStarrManagement@gmail.com
allstarrmanagement.com

Kennedy Davenport
Female Impersonator

Kennedy Davenport is an entertainer currently residing in Dallas, Texas. She had previously lived in Ft. Lauderdale, Florida where she Was featured at places like J's Bar. In 2013, Kennedy was featured on 'America's Got Talent' on NB. For Booking Information and Details Contact: All Starr Management Office: (678) 383-9902 Email: AllStarrManagement@gmail.com allstarrmanagement.com

Kings for a Cause
A National Fundraising Movement

Established in 2008 by Anson Reign, Kings for a Cause is a nationwide event in August raising money and awareness of Kings as entertainers on both the local and national levels.

Kris del Vayze
Drag Queen

International Drag Queen, Hos satirist & parodist, comedian.

Krystal Monroe Knights
Female Impersonator

If you are not having a good time doing this bow out NOW.

Landon Cider
Male Impersonator

Landon Cider is one of the Nation's leading Drag King Entertainers, mastering the makeup and impersonations of Celebrities, Movie Characters, and numerous characters of his own creation. For Booking Information and Details Contact:

All Starr Management Office: (678) 383-9902
Email: AllStarrManagement@gmail.com
allstarrmanagement.com
landoncider.com DragKing based in Los Angeles, CA, USA.

Let's Have a Fefe
Award Winning Internet Radio Show
Let's Have a Fefe is an award-winning
weekly webcast hosted by Felicia Minor and Freddy Prinze Charming. Broadcast live every Wednesday at 8pm Arizona time from YouTube.com/divaminor. Facebook.com/letshaveafefe or on Twitter @LetsHaveAFefe

Liquid
Nightclub / Show venue
1811 N 15th St, Tampa, FL 33605

Lashauwn Beyond
Female Impersonator
A successful drag designer and seamstress, this baby queen is ready for her shot in the spotlight. Equal parts goofy and shy, Lashauwn doesn't take herself too seriously. But don't be fooled by her quiet nature, this diva is known as the silent killer. Avoid getting in her crosshairs at all costs.
For Booking Information and Details
Contact: All Starr Management
Office: (678) 383-9902
Email: AllStarrManagement@gmail.com
allstarrmanagement.com

Latrice Royale
Female Impersonator

I am a California native that was born in the early seventies. I have been studying and perfecting the art of Female Impersonation for over 20 years. My career began with a dare and it was during that first performance I became hooked. Since my beginning, I have worked extensively and primarily within the State of Florida. While I have won various local titles and crowns in Florida, I believe that it is now time. It is time for me "Latrice Royale" to spread these wings a bit further. Most people that have never seen Latrice Royale perform; want to know what they are getting themselves into when they book Latrice Royale for a show. Well first and foremost it is important to understand that a show by Latrice Royale is no ordinary show.

For Booking Information and Details Contact: All Starr Management Office: (678) 383-9902

Email: AllStarrManagement@gmail.com allstarrmanagement.com

Lola Honey
Female impersonator

Lola Honey is the Antelope Valley's Premiere Drag entertainer and self-proclaimed "Queen of the California Desert." She runs her own show at "The Back Door' in Lancaster, CA. The Show has been running over ten years, 4 of which Lola has been the Host. Lola Honey has been involved in several TV/Movie projects including Dick Clark's Rocking New Year's Eve Special, The Casting Special of RuPaul Drag Race season 3, and Rampart starring Woody Harrelson. She has performed in cities thought out the west coast including Long Beach, San Francisco, Los Angeles, Seattle, Las Vegas and more.

Luke Ateraz

Mr King of the Desert USofA MI 1st alt 2013; Mr King NCC 1st alt 2013; Riverside, CA and Phoenix, AZ

Lycess Lee SparxX
Pop Diva

Madam Diva Divine

Hello, there I am Madam Diva Divine. I have been doing drag for the better part of 10 years. I started my career in Rocky Horror Picture Show shadow cast and moved quickly into the NYC nightlife. I have worked on a number of shows all across NYC and Long Island as well as parts of Florida. I enjoy hosting shows and helping raise money for benefits. Please contact me if you are looking for a seasoned hostess and performer.

Madame LaQueer
Female Impersonator
          For Booking Information and Details Contact:
All Starr Management Office: (678) 383-9902
Email: AllStarrManagement@gmail.com
allstarrmanagement.com

MadeForAQueen.com
<Advertisement on page fourteen and fifteen.>
Business
          Handmade Swarovski Austrian Crystal
Jewelry by the one and only Lucinda Holliday.

Mama Savannah Georgia
Drag Queen Comedian
          Comedy Queen for 21 years, have my own TV nWeb AWARD winning talk show "MAMA KNOWS BEST TALK SHOW" over 1 million weekly viewers, been in 2 movies, wrote for a prestigious gay men's magazine in London as "MAMA", hold titles, performed all over USA & Europe.

Michelle Leigh Sterling
Female Impersonator

Michelle Leigh Sterling comes to us from the little town of Pine Grove, PA. She has been a staple in the Harrisburg gay community, and this year, 2013, she celebrates 20 years of performing the art of female impersonation. She is known for her comedy mixes, creating her own wardrobe, and for being known as Pa's "Jewelry Whore". She has accumulated 11 titles with the title of Miss Pennsylvania America 1999 being her most cherished. She was a promoter for the Miss Pennsylvania America Pageant for five years, was nominated for best state preliminary, and honored to become the Promoter of the Year for the 2010 pageant season.
For booking information, Michellester32@hotmail.com.

Mike Oxready
King

Vermont-based Drag King
Mike Oxready got his start in co-founded troupe, New Cocks on the Block (no longer performing together), and is back on the solo king scene with creative, unique genderplay performances.
Available for bookings through email or facebook©:
mikeoxready@gmail.com

Miss Behave
Queen

Miss Behave! She is young, sassy and international. She is Germany's #1 "It Queen" and although she is new to Drag, debuting on Diva Deluxe Pageant in Frankfurt, Germany, she sure knows how to be in everybody's mouth.

MillionHugs.com

Ground zero for any performer wishing to write her memoirs or any writer needing to share a tale. Specializing in first time authors. MillionHugs.com is the direct marketplace for BecHavn Publishing (BecHavn.com), sole publisher of all the DRAG411 books. Sole owner: Todd Kachinski Kottmeier

Miss Fame
Female Impersonator
Beautiful, confident, powerful, hilarious, condemned-to-hell, divorcée, Linda-Evangelistian Super-Model.
For Booking Information and Details
Contact: All Starr Management
Office: (678) 383-9902
Email: AllStarrManagement@gmail.com
allstarrmanagement.com

Moanalot Fontaine
Entertainer

I have been a DRAG performance Artist since the 80s I started my venture in the DRAG World by raising money to help during the 80s when HIV/AID was discovered. My career took off from there. I have performed all over Southern California. I helped form a Group call the Barbitchuates. We were very big HIV/AIDS ADVOCATES RAISING MONIES IN THE EARLY 2000S MY CAREER HAS NOW BROUGHT ME TO NEW ORLEANS WHERE WE HAVE BROUGHT OUR GROUP THE BARBITCHUATES HERE. I also am cofounder of the BIG EASY SISTER A MISSION HOUSE OF THE SISTERS OF PERPETUAL INDULGENCE I AM ABBESS OF OUR HOUSE MY NAME AS A SISTER IS NVS SR SISTER MOANA MOANSALOTTS. We have our monthly Barbitchuates Show here in NOLA and the Sisters have monthly fundraisers. So this is brief description of what I do.

Monica Beverly Hillz
Female Impersonator
For Booking Information and Details Contact:
All Starr Management Office: (678) 383-9902
Email:
AllStarrManagement@gmail.com
allstarrmanagement.com

Morgan McMichael
Female Impersonator
For Booking Information and Details
Contact: All Starr Management Office:
(678) 383-9902 Email:
AllStarrManagement@gmail.com
allstarrmanagement.com

Natasha Richards
Female Impersonator

Growing up In New York City, my grandmother (an original Radio City Music Hall Rockette) brought us to the Hamptons while my mother sprint to the gay bars. As I grew older, I began to think, "I WANT TO BE QUEEN OF THE WORLD." I began teaching Ballroom at the local Arthur Murray Dance Studio. The lessons I learned through their discipline and a knack for costumes sent me on a journey that eventually led to becoming the youngest Miss Gay USofA in history (24), after four exciting attempts. My path brought me again to the crown for Miss National 2003 and thirty-six other titles. Now, I am an advocate for AIDS Partnership, Inc. a nonprofit 501 (c)(3) resource for groups and/or individuals (aidspartnershipinc.com), co-hosting with Traila Park our own Bingo Charity Fundraiser, with over $30,000 in donations to date and growing. I hope to inspire those seeking to be fabulous by sharing my spirit.

Nostalgia Todd Ronin
Female Impersonator

Up and coming entertainer currently based out of Jacksonville, FL. Willing to travel for the right opportunity or circumstance. Known for retro, comedy/camp, club kid, genderf*ck, and spooky drag. I have no known limits when it comes to challenges, variety, and entertainment value.

Old Street Saloon
Bar/nightclub

Smaller, friendly club with drag shows on the weekends. Karaoke on the 1st and 3rd Fridays. Very well known for its quality drag shows.

Pandora DeStrange
Drag Queen

Pandora DeStrange leaves quite an impression wherever she goes! She gives a performance that is raw, edgy and rambunctious. With a gravelly, rock and roll voice reminiscent of Wendy O. Williams and the defiant attitude of Boy George, she rules the stage. Whether she's singing a bawdy parody or a heartfelt ballad her artistry shines through. This Punk Rock Princess takes the term "Flaming Queen" to a whole new level.

Papa Cherry
Male impersonator

Papa Cherry is a drag king performer as well as te producer for LA's hottest drag show – BENT

Phoenix
Female Impersonator
For Booking Information and Details Contact: All Starr Management Office: (678) 383-9902 Email: AllStarrManagement@gmail.com allstarrmanagement.com

Email: AllStarrManagement@gmail.com
allstarrmanagement.com

Porcelain
Female Impersonator

Porcelain is as edgy as they come. She has a unique style all her own, constantly pushing the boundaries of drag. Those piercing eyes, the big cheekbones, the sharp eye brows, and the big poisonous lips- that is Porcelain, "Queen of the Damned". This talented young Philly-based goddess does not just have the looks to kill, but the performing skills to match. She demands the crowd's attention with her suspensions, fire swallowing, and pole acrobatics. For Booking Information and Details Contact: All Starr Management Office:

PurrZsa Kyttyn Azrael
Queen
        PurrZsa transcends normalcy and the expected and is known as "the craziest cat in captivity" Derived from a theatrical background, I am first and foremost an entertainer and you never know what is going to happen next.

Queens of Detroit, Past, Present, and Future
A facebook© group
        A place to get the latest information on performers in Michigan Past, Present, and Future

Rainbow411.com
On line gay friendly search
Your Life • Your Needs •
Your Source for everything Gay Friendly!
Created for our passion for the GLBT
community. Rainbow411
connects individuals
with gay friendly businesses. If you know
of a gay friendly business please refer
them to info@rainbow411.com

Raja
Female Impersonator
        Legendary Los Angeles Artist Model Muse Performer Winner of RuPaul's Drag Race Season 3. Exotic and edgy. Raja has the other queens gagging at more than just her eleganza. A self-professed supermodel, Raja is setting the runway on fire with her ferocious strut and eye-popping style. Stand in her wayand Raja will shantay past you like fashion road kill. For Booking Information and Details Contact: All Starr Management Office: (678) 383-9902 Email: AllStarrManagement@gmail.com allstarrmanagement.com

Raquel Blake
Female Impersonator
        For Booking Information and Details Contact: All Starr Management Office: (678) 383-9902 Email: AllStarrManagement@gmail.com allstarrmanagement.com

Rasta Boi Punany

Rochelle L. Johnson AKA Rasta Boi Punany. I am an African-descent Drag King who hails from East Orange, New Jersey and has taken Philadelphia, Pennsylvania by storm. I entered the profession in April 2011 as a contestant in the Mr.Philadelphia Drag King competition and won. That lead me to also winning the Mr. Philadelphia Gay Pride title and since then I have won Mr. Divo International M.I. and Mr. Pennsylvania Ultimate King. I have enjoyed every minute of my time and enjoy entertaining and meeting new people and other performers. I appreciate the community and I do my best to give back. Thank you and enjoy.

Rasta Boi Punany

Volunteered for Action AIDS, done fundraisers as a performer throughout the city of Philadelphia (too many to name), traveled to Missouri, Pittsburgh, Columbus and Cleveland, Ohio, sponsored events including the Philadelphia's Trans-Gender Conference (and performed), Southern Jersey LGBTQ National Coming Out Day, and Atlantic City's National Coming Out Day.

She volunteered for Philly's DykeMarch, Philly Outfest, Philly Pride annual events, and is a member of the Elegance Family. This performer participated in the Philadelphia Transgender March and hopes as a Drag King to take their skills to South Africa. In life, she is a family therapist and licensed social worker, individually counseling men, women, and children of all ages, race, and sexual orientation She continues to support the rights of all, as both the former Board member and Outreach member of Elements Organization, for LGBTQ Women of Color.

Photo by Freedom G Photography

RuPaul
Female Impersonator
        Looking to hire Rupaul? To contact a booking agent for RuPaul or to get pricing, fees and availability for RuPaul to perform at your corporate event, gala,
fundraiser, private party, public concert, wedding, college, fair or festival? Give us a call at (212) 645-0555.   bookingentertainment.com

Ruby Diamond NY
Female Impersonator
        I have a strong belief in Anti-bullying...I will stand up and be a voice. I put on shows to bring joy to people to forget all issues even if for a little while.   I can also do private shows for a fee contact me at Rubydiamond1979@gmail.com or on Facebook©.

Sabrina Kayson
Female impersonator
        Miss Knoxville Drag Idol 2013-14. (865) 244-9979 facebook.com/SabrinaKayson

Sasha Stephen
Female impersonator
        Contact me at athensbitch@yahoo.com
Savannah Leigh
Female Impersonator
        For Booking Information and Details
Contact: All Starr Management Office: (678) 383-9902
Email: AllStarrManagement@gmail.com
allstarrmanagement.com

Serenity St Clair
Queen
        I am Serenity St Clair. I've been performing in the business for seven years, and love every minute I get to serve the community & you realness in the TN, VA, INN, and KY areas.

Shannel
Female Impersonator
        Born and raised in southern California, Bryan Watkins has been performing and dazzling audiences as Shannel, a female illusionist and drag queen for the past 18 years. At the age of 15, Bryan entered and won a Halloween contest in drag- there, Shannel was born. A year later, she began working with Glamour Shots

as a makeup artist and a hairstylist, providing her expertise on photo shoots. Soon after, she was discovered by a representative of the Chanel Corporation and was hired on as a beauty advisor for Chanel cosmetic. Shannel's career took off and she resided in Las Vegas as a host and headliner for over 9 years. In 2009, she was cast in the first season of Logo's RuPaul's Drag Race. After noticeable recognition from the show,Shannel returned to Southern California and continued touring around the United States. In 2012, she was chosen to be on RuPaul's Drag Race: All Stars. 2013 has been a very busy year for Shannel. In March, she became a part of CeeLo Green's "LOberace" at Planet Hollywood on the Las Vegas Strip. As springtime finished, it was announced that she will be a reoccurring co-host with Frank Marino and his Las Vegas show "Divas". Currently, she continues to travel and work with the Dreamgirls Revue Shows and special guest appearances in clubs all around the U.S. For Booking Information and Details Contact: All Starr Management Office: (678) 383-9902 Email: AllStarrManagement@gmail.com allstarrmanagement.com

Shaunna Rai
Female Impersonator
          Available   for   shows/bookings   around   New   England bluevirgo72@yahoo.com

Starr Mirage Cummings
 Female Impersonator
          A drag performer from Uniontown, Pennsylvania. She has been performing across the tri-state area for the last five years.

Stephanie Stuart
Female impersonator
          Living and working in west central Florida available for bookings and travel

Stilettos
Nightclub / Show venue
          Stilettos is the hottest and most exciting nightclub for the gay and lesbian community in Detroit, Michigan. Showcasing two unique bars under one roof, you can either choose to enjoy top entertainment along with a diverse crowd, or dance the night away in the heart-pumping, wild women's ADRENALINE ROOM!

Summer Rayne
Female Impersonator
          New Orleans only "Celine Dion" impersonator. Summer can be booked for private functions as well as corporate events, pageants, and shows. Email summerrayneproductions@gmail.com for rates.

Temptation
Female impersonator
        865-235-6674

Taina Norell
Female Impersonator
        Hello Guys , My name is Taina...26 year transsexual actress & model born in the beautiful island of Cuba. Interested in: Plays (Broadway style), Photo shoots, Modeling, and Acting. Booking Information and Details Contact: All Starr Management Office: (678) 383-9902 Email: AllStarrManagement@gmail.com allstarrmanagement.com

Tiffani T. Middlesexx
Writer / Female
Impersonator

The Bromantics
Drag King Troupe
        Montreal's finest (and only) troupe of drag kings!   FB: The Bromantics : Montreal Drag Kings   E-mail: bromanticsmtl@gmail.com

Tsunami Foxx
Drag Queen
Contact me through roseempress52@gmail.com

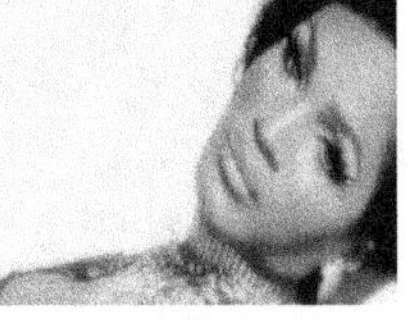

Trinity K. Bonet
Female Impersonator
        For Booking Information and Details
Contact: All Starr Management Office: (678) 383-9902
Email: AllStarrManagement@gmail.com
allstarrmanagement.com

Twila Starr
Queen
        In the business for 40 yrs. started with Ms. Tiffini Middllesexx our friendship still remains very strong. I have worked in Toledo for yrs. and have won countless titles but they were local titles I have my shot and the larger ones the highest I got was runner up ijn a miss gay Ohio America from then on I surrendered pageants and decided to do something more worthwhile in our community aids was a new epidemic and everyone was on pins and needles I lost so many dear friends in that period that I decided to do something about it they had no money

and government funding was small thus started small fundraiser "That What Friends are For" started with me by another dear friend Alexis winter we had a wonderful turn out and that was for a nonprofit called nova then it switched to David's house a hospice for sick patients I missed the first 2 but decided to attend 3 and 4 and then at the 5th one I was asked to perform ! at the 5th one as a surprise none of the board members knew when I came out I tore the house down it was at the amphitheater at the zoo it will always be memorable I've done so much in the fight against aids and so many other diseases I am the Diva of Toledo and still remain Long Live the Queen.

Tyra Sanchez
Female Impersonator

Tyra is best known as the winner of the second season of RuPaul's Drag Race. A native of Gainesville, Florida, Ross moved to Orlando, where he resided for most of his life. During his time on RuPaul's Drag Race, Ross spoke candidly about his periods of homelessness and personal challenges prior to auditioning for and being selected to appear on the show. Ross' old-school drag style and glamor made him a favorite of the judges although his acerbic personality earned him the disdain of his fellow contestants. Currently residing in Atlanta, Ross performs throughout the United States and Canada. At the time he won the title, Ross was one of the youngest contestants to appear on RuPaul's Drag Race; he was also one of the few contestants on the show who never had to lip sync in order to avoid elimination prior to the season finale. In June 2012, it was announced that a documentary film called, "Drag Dad," will begin filming discussing Ross's role as a father. For Booking Information and Details Contact: All Starr Management Office: (678) 383-9902 Email: AllStarrManagement@gmail.com allstarrmanagement.com

Venus D'Lite
Female Impersonator

Adam Guerra (born September 5, 1983), known as Venus D'Lite, is an actor-performer famous for his drag queen persona. Venus hit the scene with his drag performances in 2002 and quickly secured notoriety as the preeminent Madonna impersonator of our time. He has appeared in a variety of television programs, films, and music videos. Venus was featured contestant on Season 3 of the reality television show, RuPaul's Drag Race. Venus D'Lite was born in Los Angeles. His name was inspired by the 1986 Bananarama it cover song "Venus". Growing up, Venus was heavily influenced by the music and pop culture of the '80s. His mother was responsible for exposing Venus to icons such as Marilyn Monroe, Liza Minnelli, Madonna, Grace Jones, and Barbara Streisand. He was also influenced by the musical Cabaret while growing up. His fascination with Marilyn Monroe and Madonna paved the road to his success as one of the industry's most talented drag performers. Venus first hit the stage in drag with a Marilyn impersonation in 2002, marking the 40th anniversary of Monroe's death. This performance led to Venus appearing as Marilyn on the reality sitcom: The Anna Nicole Smith show. Admirers soon began to draw parallels between Venus and his childhood idol Madonna due to physical similarities. His extraordinary ability to transform into Madonna made him enormously popular in the Southern California gay scene. The newfound fame led to Venus appearing on the daytime talk show Ricki Lake where she performed Madonna's "Like a Virgin". Venus later went on to appear in Christiana Aguilera's video "Hurt" in 2006. This was followed with a role in the 2007 satirical comedy "The Comebacks" which to this date is the only motion picture featuring a Madonna female impersonator. D'Lite is currently the youngest cast member of the acclaimed drag show: The Dreamgirls Revue and performs frequently at several Los Angeles gay clubs. In December 2010, Venus will be start in a new holiday-themed play by Tony Blass, Madonna's Christmas Carol, in which the famed impersonator will star as the Material Girl. For Booking Information and Details Contact: All Starr Management Office: (678) 383-9902 Email: AllStarrManagement@gmail.com allstarrmanagement.com

Vinnie Marconi
Male impersonator

Male Illusionist, Tampa Bay, FL
Photo by Alex Melo, 2013 Winner of DRAG411's Peer Award for "Best Drag King Photographer"

Vita DeVine
Queen
    I bring a variety of acts that appeal to all audiences. I try to energize the crowd and entertain them.

Vivian Von Brokenhymen
Queen
    Vivian is known for her fabulous costumes, campy humor and witty repartee on the microphone.

Vivikah Kayson-Raye
Female impersonator

Entertainer from Knoxville, Tennessee   Miss Tennessee USA Unlimited Newcomer 2012 Miss Southern States Unlimited Newcomer 2013 Show Director and Emcee at Kristtopher's in Knoxville, Tennessee

Wendy G Kennedy
Drag Queen

I am Wendy G Kennedy. I'm more than meets the eye and a Drag Queen with passion willing to help our LGBT Community in any way possible

Witti Repartee
Queen   Singer, dancer, hostess and philanthropist

Witti Repartee is a queen for all communities! Whether at drag balls, on the stage of bars and other venues, in the leather or bear communities, she has often found helping to raise money for LGBT and HIV org

Writing the Vision, LLC
Business

Purchase your copy of 100 of the Most Influential Gay Entertainers, Volumes I and II at www.100mige.com (autographed copies) or lulu.com/shop.

Yara Sofia
Female Impersonator

My name is Gabriel Burgos better known as Yara Sofia. I was born on May 8, 1984 in San Juan, Puerto Rico. I always had shown interest in theatrical arts and dancing. I have a bachelor's degree in Drama and an associate's degree in Fashion Design and Haute couture. This was the main reason why I decided to started developing myself as an actor and at the same time, I worked creating costumes for plays at Sacred Heart University of Puerto Rico.

In 2005 I won my first crown as "Miss Road To Diva" Krash The Club. By 2010, I decided to take my drag career to another level so I decided to audition for the famous TV show: "Rupaul's Drag Race" transmitted in Logo and Vh1. I was 4th runner up and voted for people's choice as Miss Congeniality. I recently moved to Los Angeles expecting to keep growing as a performer and get to know in the world of fashion.

For Booking Information and Details Contact: All Starr Management Office: (678) 383-9902 Email: AllStarrManagement@gmail.com allstarrmanagement.com

Ten Black Books

Book 1   DRAG411's
"DRAG Bully, A Survivor's Guide"

The Largest Bullying Project in LGBT History for Struggling Entertainers. Advice from over a hundred male, female, and androgynous impersonators around the world to help entertainers struggling with their family, peers, relationships, neighbors, regular jobs, venues, and successfully overcoming self-doubt. Best Selling author Todd Kachinski Kottmeier created DRAG411 to document the lives of male, female, and androgynous impersonator years ago. It is now the largest organization for impersonators on earth with over 7,000 entertainers in 32 countries. DRAG411 also operates The International Original, Official DRAG Memorial with almost a thousand names (2018). This is his 25th book, 20th World Record, and 12th book on this subject. Thousands of invitations to contribute were send out. This book contains the best of their responses, in their own words, to you.

Book 2 DRAG411's
"Original DRAG Handbook"

Over 155 female impersonators (and 1 male impersonator) from around the world share over a thousand insightful comments in the first handbook created of this art form.

Commentary shared with Todd Kachinski Kottmeier included the following contributors of The Original, DRAG Handbook to include Ada Buffet, Adora , Adrian Leigh, Afeelya Bunz, Alisa Summers, Alanna Divine, Alexis De La Mer, Alexis Mateo, Alex Serpa, Allure, Amanda Bone, Amanda Love, Amy DeMilo, Anastaia Fallon, Astasnaia Rexia, Angel gLamar, Angela Dodd, Anita Cox, April Fresh, Ashleigh Cooley, Aurora Sexton, Babette Schwartz, Bailey St. James, Barbra Herr, Barbra Seville, Beverly LaSalle, BJ Stephens, Blair Michaels, Brandon M. Caten, Brianna Lee, Brittany Moore, Brookyln Bisette, Bukkake Blaque London St. James, Cartier Paris, Cathy Craig, Champagne T. Bordeaux, Cherry Darling, Christina Paris, CoCo LaBelle, CoCo Montrese, CoCo St. James, Conundrum, Crystal Belle, Daniel Murphy, Danika Fierce, Daphne Ferraro, Dasha Nicole, Dee Gregory, Deva DaVyne, Diamond Dunhill, Diedra Windsor Walker, Dmentia Divinyl/Eva LaDeva, Echo Dazz, Esme Russell, Estelle Rivers, Funyce Raye, Felica Fox, Felina Cashmere, Geraldine Queen Cabaret, Ginger Minj, Glitz Glam, Gilda Golden, Horchata, Ima Twat, Ineeda Twat, Jade Daniels, Jade Jolie, Jade Shanell, Jade Sotomayo, Jaeda Fuentes, Jami Micheals, Jay Santana, Jeffrey Powell, Jenna Chambers Tisdale, Jessica Jade, Jocelyn Summers, Jodie Holliday, Joey Brooks, Joshua Myers, J.P. Patrick, Juwanna Jackson, Kamden Wells, Katrina Starr, Kenny Braverman, Khrystal Leight, Kier Sarkesian, Kiki LaFlare Santangilo, Kitty D'Meaner, Kori Stevens, Krystal Amore Adonis, Lacey Lynn Taylors, Lady Clover Honey, Lady Sabrina, Lady TaJma Hall, Lakeisha Pryce, LeeAnna Love, Leigh Shannon, Lisa Carr, Lola Honey, Madisyn De

La Mer, Makayla Rose Devine, Maxine Padlock (Maxi Pad), Melissa Morgan, Melody Mayheim, Michael Wilson, Mike Astermon-Glidden, Mis Sadistic, Miss Conception, Miss Gigi, Mr. Kenneth Blake, Misty Eyez, Monique Michaels, Myah Monroe, Mystique Summers, Nairobi V. D'Viante, Naomi D-Lish, Naomi Wynters, Nicole Paige Brooks, Nikki Dynamite, Nova Starr, Ororo, Patrica Grand, Patricia Knight, Patrica Mason, Pandora DeStrange, Penelope Reigns, Polly FunkChanel, Phiore Star Liemont, Purrzsa Kyttyn, Pussy LeHoot, Raquel Payne, Rhyana Vorhman, Rickie Lee, Rusti Fawcett, Scarlett Fever, Selina Kyle, Shae Shae LaReese, Shealita Babay, Shugah Caine, Stephanie Roberts, Stephanie Stuart, Stormy Vain, Summer Breeze, Sybil Storm, Tabatha Lovall, Tatum Michelle, Teri Courtney, Tiffani Middlesexx, Timm McBride, Toni Davyne, TotiYanah Diamond,Trixie LaRue, Trixie Pleasures, Vegas Platinum, Venus D Lite, Vivika D'Angelo, Wendel Duppert and Wendy G. Kennedy.

Book 3:   DRAG411's
"Crown Me! Winning Pageants"

Hundreds of invitations sent to the titleholders, pageant promoters, judges, and talent show hosts to share their insight on not only winning pageants and contests but also owning the stage every time they perform. Their topics included auxiliary steps to success needed for song selection, dancing, movement on stage, props, backup dancers, creating your own edge, personal interviews, steps to success for winning the talent category every time you step on stage, on stage questions, eveningwear, and creative costuming. They discussed in their own unedited words, wardrobe changes, makeup, hair, shoes, when is the time to compete, qualities needed for a judge, and the top misconceptions of contestants competing in the pageantry systems.

Commentary shared with Todd Kachinski Kottmeier included the following contributors of Crown Me! to include AJ Menendez, Amy Demilo, Anastacia Dupree, Anson Reign, Bob Taylor, Breonna Tenae, Brittany T Moore, Coco Montrese, Dana Douglas, Darryl Kent, Denise Russell, Dey Jzah Opulent, Freddy Prinze Charming, Gage Gatlyn, Jay Santana , Jayden Knight, Jennifer Foxx, Joey Jay, Kori Stevens, Mis Sadistic, Mykul Jay Valentine, Natasha Richards, Rico Taylor, Sam Hare, Stephanie Stuart, Taina T. Norell, Tiffani Middlesexx, Tori Taylor, Ty Nolan, Vinnie Marconi, and Vivika D'Angelo.

Book 4:   DRAG411's
"DRAG King Guide"

Over 155 male impersonators around the world share over a thousand insightful comments in forty-one chapters.

Commentary shared with Todd Kachinski Kottmeier included the following contributors of The Official DRAG King and Male Impersonators Guide to include Aaron Phoenix, Abs Hart, Adam All, Adam DoEve, AJ Menendez, Alec Allnight, Alexander Cameron, Alik Muf, Andrew Citino, Anjie Swidergal, Anson Reign, Ashton The Adorable Lover, Atown, Ayden Layne, B J Armani, B J Bottoms, Bailey Saint James, Ben Doverr, Ben Eaten, Bootzy Edwards Collynz, Brandon KC Young-Taylor, Bruno Diaz, Cage Masters, Campbell Reid Andrews, Chance Wise, Chandler J Hart, Chasin Love, Cherry Tyler

Manhattan, Chris Mandingo, Clark Kunt, Clint Torres, Cody Wellch Klondyke, Colin Grey, Corey James Caster, Coti Blayne, Crash Bandikok, Dakota Rain, Dante Diamond, Davion Summers, DeVery Bess, Devin G. Dame, Devon Ayers, Dionysus W Khaos, Diseal Tanks Roberts, D-Luv

Saviyon, Dominic Demornay, Dominic Von Strap, D-Rex, Dylan Kane, E. M. Shaun, Eddie C. Broadway, Emilio, Erick LaRue, Flex Jonez, Freddy Prinze Charming, Gabe King, Gage Gatlyn, George De Micheal, Greyson Bolt, Gunner Gatlyn, Gus Magendor, Hawk Stuart, Harry Pi, Holden Michael, Howie Feltersnatch, Hurricane Savage, J Breezy St James, Jack E. Dickinson, Jack King, Jake Van Camp, Jamel Knight, Jenson C. Dean, Johnnie Blackheart, Jonah Godfather of DRAG, Jordan Allen, Jordan Reighn, Joshua K. Mann, Joshua Micheals, Juan Kerr, Julius M. SeizeHer, Jude Lawless, Justin Cider, Justin Luvan, Justin Sider, K'ne Cole, Kameo Dupree, Kenneth J. Squires, King Dante, King Ramsey, Jack Inman, Kody Sky, Koomah, Kristian Kyler, Kruz Mhee, Linda Hermann-Chasin, Luke Ateraz, Lyle Love-It, Macximus, Marcus Mayhem, Marty Brown, Master Cameron Eric Leon, Max Hardswell, MaXx Decco, Michael Christian, Mike Oxready, Miles Long, Mr-Charlie Smith, Nanette D'angelo Sylvan, Nolan Neptune, Orion Blaze Browne, Owlejandro Monroe, Papa Cherry, Papi Chulo, Papi Chulo Doll, Persian Prince, Phantom, Pierce Gabriel, Rasta Boi Punany, Rico M Taylor, Rock McGroyn, Rocky Valentino, Rogue DRAG King, Romeo Sanchez, Rychard "Alpha" Le'Sabre, Ryder Knightly, Ryder Long, Sam Masterson, Sammy Silver, Santana Romero, Scorpio, Shane Rebel Caine, Shook ByNature, Silk Steele Prince, SirMandingo Thatis, Smitty O'Toole, Soco Dupree, Spacee Kadett, Starr Masters, Stefan LeDude, Stefon Royce Iman, Stefon SanDiego, Stormm, Teddy Michael, Thug Passion, Travis Luvermore, Travis Hard, Trey C. Michaels, Trigger Montgomery,   Tyler Manhattan, Viciouse Slick, Vinnie Marconi, Welland Dowd, William Vanity Matrix, Wulf Von Monroe, Xander Havoc, and Xavier Bottoms.

Book 5:   DRAG411's
"DRAG Stories"

Funny stories shared with Todd Kachinski Kottmeier including the following contributors of DRAG Stories to include Chance Wise, Anson Reign, Tiffani Middlesexx, Rico Taylor, Todd Kachinski Kottmeier, Bob Taylor, Stefon Royce Iman, Candi Samples, Alexis Mateo, Naomi Wynters, Dmentia Divinyl, Bruce Lacie, Kennedy Wendy, Chastity Rose, Miss GiGi, Angel gLamar, Patricia Grand, Shook ByNature, Lady Guy, Eunyce Raye, Charley Marie Coutora, Jezzie Bell, Lamar Kellam, Jayden St. James, Rachelle Ann Summers, Champagne T Bordeaux, Gilda Golden, Daisha Monet, Vivika D'Angelo, Rachel Boheme, Esme Rodriguez, and MaNu Da Original.

Book 6:   DRAG411's
"DRAG Mother, DRAG Father" Honoring Mentors

Performers look to DRAG mothers, DRAG fathers, friends, and fans for insight, compassion, and guidance as mentors. This book honors those special people. Over 140 entertainers contributed wisdom and words for this historical book, making it the largest project of its nature in GLBTQ history and the first published book on male and female mentors.

Commentary shared with Todd Kachinski Kottmeier included the following contributors of DRAG Parents to includee AJ Menendez, Vinnie Marconi, Mis Sadistic, Todd Kachinski Kottmeier, Bob Taylor, Taina Norell, Andrew Stratton, Horchata Horchata, David Warner, Gianna Love, Trinity Taylor, Domunique Jazmin Vizcaya, Brittany Moore, PurrZsa Kyttyn, Jake Lickur, Shelita Taylor, Adriana Manchez, MiMi Welch, China Taylor, Armondis Bone't, Monique Trudeau, Simeon Codfish, Diamond Dupree, Stefon Royce Iman, Jayden Stjames, Demonica da Bomb, Colin Grey, Christopher Todd Guy, Celyndra Lashay Clyne, Candice St. James, Justin Barnes Williams, Ivanna Dooche, London Taylor Douglas, Christina Alexandria Victoria Regina Lowe, Bianca DeMonet, Critiqa Mann, Jazmen Andrews, AJ Allen, TotiYanah Diamond, D' Marco Knight, Chip Matthews, Mirage Montrese, India Starr Simms, Jade S Stratton, Emerald Divine, Elysse Giovanni, Vanity Halston, Kristofer Reynolds, Akasha Uravitch, Adriana Fuentes, Erykah Mirage, Felicity Ferraro, Joey Payge, Rhiannon Todd, Vicious Slick, Amirage Saling, Tori Sass, Chy'enne Valentino, and Robbi Lynn.

Book 7:   DRAG411's
"Spotlight Today"

It was the World's Largest Paperback Magazine for Impersonators and Fans when it premiered with over 175 pages. DRAG411 no longer prints Spotlight Today Magazine, but here is the re-release of the groundbreaking first edition. Complete articles by Vinnie Marconi, Denise Russell, Tiffani T. Middlesexx, Kristofer Reynolds, Magenta Alexandria Dupree, Butch Daddy, Vivikah Kayson-Raye, Makanoe, Amanda Lay, Thomas DeVoyd, Kevin B. Reed, Glenn Storm, and over 150 impersonators from around the world.

Book 8:   DRAG411's
"DRAG Queen Guide"

Almost two hundred female impersonators around the world share over a thousand insightful comments in forty-one chapters.

Commentary shared with Todd Kachinski Kottmeier included the following contributors of Official DRAG Queen and Female Impersonator Handbook to include Alana Summers, Alexis Marie Von Furstenburg, Alize', Aloe Vera, Alysin Wonderland, Amanda Bone DeMornay, Amanda Lay, Amanda Roberts, Amy DeMilo, Anastasia Fallon, Angie Ovahness, Anita Mandinite, Appolonia Cruz, Ashlyn Tyler, Aurora Tr'Nele Michelle, Azia Sparks, Barbie Dayne, Barbra Herr, Beverly LaSalle, Bianca DeMonet, Bianca Lynn Breeze, Blair Michaels, Boxxa Vine, Brittany T Moore, Britney Towers, Brandi Amara Skyy, Brooke Lynn Bradshaw, Candi Samples, Candi Stratton, Candy

Sugar, Cathy Craig, Catia Lee Love, CeCe Georgia, Cee-Cee LaRouge-Avalon, Celeste Starr, Chad Michaels, Chevon Davis, Cheyenne Desoto Mykels, Chi Chi Lalique, Christina Collins, Chrystal Conners, Claudia B Eautiful, Coca Mesa, Coco St James, Damiana LaRoux, Dana Scrumptious, Danyel Vasquez, Dee Gregory, Delores T. Van-Cartier, Demonica DaBaum, Denise Russell, Diamond Dunhill, Diva Lilo, Diva Savage, Dove, EdriAna Treviño, Elle Emenopé, Elysse Giovanni, Erica James, Esmé Rodríguez, Estella Sweet, Eunyce Raye, Eva Nichole Distruction, Faleasha Savage, Felicia Minor, Felicity Frockaccino, Gigi Masters, Ginger Alley, Ginger Gigi Diamond, Ginger Kaye Belmont, Glitz Glam, Grecia Montes D' Occa, Heather Daniels, Hennessy Heart, Hershae Chocolatae, Holy McGrail, Hope B Childs, Horchata, India Brooks, India Ferrah, Ivy Profen, Izzy Adahl, Jaclyn St James, Jade Iroq, Jade Sotomayor, Jade Taylor Stratton, Jamie-Ree Swan, Jennifer Warner, Jessica Brooks, Jexa Ren'ae Van de Kamp, Joey Brooks, Jonny Pride, Kamelle Toe, Karma Jayde Addams, Kelly Turner, Mama Savannah Georgia, Mr. Kenneth Blake, Kamden T. Rage, Kira Stone-St James, Kirby Kolby, Kita Rose, Krysta Radiance, Lacie Bruce, Lady Jasmine Michaels, Lady Pearl, Lady Sabrina, Latrice Royale, LaTonga Manchez, Leona Barr, Lexi Alexander, Lilo Monroe, Lindsay Carlton, Lucinda Holliday, Lunara Sky, Lupita Chiquita Michaels Alexander, Madam Diva Divine, Mahog Anny, Makayla Michelle Davis Diamond, Mariah Cherry, Maxine Padlock, Melody Mayheim, Menaje E'toi, Mercede Andrews, Mi$hal, Mia Fierce, Michelle Leigh Sterling, Miss Diva Savage, Miss GiGi,

Misty Eyez, Mitze Peterbilt, Monica Mystique, Montrese Lamar Hollar, Morgana DeRaven, Muffy Vanbeaverhousen, Natasha Richards, Nathan Loveland, Nicole Paige Brooks, Nikki Garcia, Nostalgia Todd Ronin, Olivia St James, Paige Sinclair, Pandora DeCeption, Pheobe James, Reia'Cheille Lucious, Robyn Demornay, Robyn Graves, Rhonda Sheer, Rose Murphy, Ruby Diamond NY, Ruby Holiday, Ryan Royale, Rychard "Alpha" Le'Sabre, Rye Seronie, Sable Monay, Sabrina Kayson-Raye, Samantha St Clair, Sanaa Raelynn, Sapphire T. Mylan, Sasha Phillips, Savannah Rivers, Savannah Stevens, Selina Kyle, Sha'day Halston-St James, ShaeShae LaReese, Shamya Banx, Shana Nicole, Shaunna Rai, Sierra Foxx White, Sierra Santana, Sonja Jae Savage, Stella D'oro, Strawberry Whip, Sugarpill, Tasha Carter, Tanna Blake, Taquella Roze, Tawdri Hipburn, Taylor Rockland, Tempest DuJour, Tiffani T. Middlesexx, Traci Russell, Trudy Tyler, Vanessa del Rey, Velveeta WhoreMel, Vera Delmar, Vicky Summers, Vita DeVine, Vivian Sorensin, Vivian Von Brokenhymen, Vivika D'Angelo-Steele, Wendy G. Kennedy, Willmuh Dickfit, Wynter Storm, Yasmine Alexander and ZuZu Bella.

Book 9:   DRAG411's (Two Comedy Scripts)
"Best Said Dead" and **"Following Wynter"**

Best Said Dead examines in funny conversations those brief minutes after a person dies. Many religions and beliefs define different paths for each of us. Rarely do we discuss those precious moments between death and the final destination. This comedy opens the possibilities that for a moment, a person vanishes into the memories in their mind. Any part can be male, female, or ambiguous.

Following Wynter is a hilarious comedy play. Ethan discovers his newlywed husband is the flamboyant DRAG queen Wynter Storm in this whimsical farce with an important message of believing in yourself and your friends. . . even if your friend is Serena Silver. Any part can be male, female, or ambiguous.

Book 10:   DRAG411's
"DRAG World"
The contributing writers of DRAG411's "Spotlight Magazine," the World's Largest Paperback Magazine for Impersonators and Fans when it premiered in 2012 with over 175 pages, created this companion book. DRAG411 no longer prints Spotlight Today Magazine, but above you will find Book 7 is the re-release of the groundbreaking first edition. Complete chapters on DRAG Marketing by DRAG411.

Complimentary articles on Confidence, Duct Tape, Music Selection, Living Divinely, authentic stage presence, Pageants, having fun performing, jewelry, legislative information from the United States and around the world, the Old School performers, Virgin stage performers, and payday from contributing writers including Denise Russell, Jay Santana, Chance Wise, Vivikah Kayson-Raye, AJ Menedez, Glenn Storm, Freddy Prinze Charming, Gage Gatlyn, Kevin B. Reed, and over 100 impersonators from around the world!

Other books from the Best Selling author
The Infamous Todd Kachinski Kottmeier

"Turn Around Bright Eyes, The DRAG Queen Killer"

Few crimes in gay history rocked a nation as great as The DRAG Queen Killer. The country seemed paralyzed from the first ring of the chain tapping on the concrete, as they pulled Cassandra to her death, until the very last brutal killing. The murderous rampage seemed buried amongst the media suffering from a barrage of tales from the 9-11 terrorist attacks.

"CommUnity of Transition"

We sent over a thousand invitations to the transgender community around the world asking them to share wisdom, advice, and compassion for those questioning or struggling. No restraints, using topics they created, as they guided the conversation over forty chapters and fifty topics. By the close, these remarkable people had created the largest compilation book in transgender history. They opened their heart with these words.

NOTE: *This book is "lightly edited" to reflect the intent and form of over one hundred transgender contributors. Unedited photographs "before and after" come from actual contributing transgender writers.*

"Joey Brooks, The Show Must Go On"
By Joey Brooks and Todd Kachinski Kottmeier

Joey Brooks, The Show Must Go On is the story of The First Lady of Ybor from the days of El Goya to present day. Female Impersonator, Show director, hostess, author…
"Old school, new school, no school… who gives a shit? I'm too old to go to school. I barely remember last week. When I get too old to remember what the fuck I did when I was young …ger, I'll just open one of these books and laugh my ass off. I wonder how many other queens had this much fun becoming one of the icons of their community. Too funny. I just called myself an icon. Hell, I must be a queen. Only a female impersonator could call themselves a diva, a queen, a star without people giggling behind her back. Giggling is good. A twenty-dollar bill is better."

"Two Days Past Dead"

The Author's First Published Book

It is hard to be the good guy when you succeed so well being bad. This is the Auggie Summer's dilemma his entire life. The story, based loosely on the tales of The Infamous Todd, follows the precocious child. His story begins with selling candy in 9th grade where he catches not only the attention of the press but also amusement of the drug cartel early in its' own infancy. Auggie Summers finds himself in the forefront of one of the most dangerous organizations on Earth.

"Waiting On God"
The Author's Humorist Novel

Learn to live after the doctors tell you "that are dying." A humorist essay on embracing funny moments and to create an environment around you that makes people not only laugh, but also be inspired by your strength.